# Secret Desires of the One Percent

*A Short Story Collection from The World's Most Notorious Madam*

## Anna Gristina

WAHIDA CLARK
PRESENTS
INNOVATIVE PUBLISHING

**Content Warning**

**This book contains subjects intended for mature audiences only. Furthermore, sensitive subjects are present in the work, including BDSM, drug use, verbal abuse, and pedophilia. Reader discretion is advised.**

Wahida Clark Presents Publishing

P.O. BOX 383

Fairburn GA 30213

1(866) 910-6920

www.wclarkpublishing.com

Library of Congress Cataloging-In-Publication Data:


Secret Desires of the One Percent

Hardcover ISBN: 978-1-957954-08-0

Paperback: 978-1-957954-09-7

Ebook ISBN: 978-1-957954-10-3

Library of Congress Control Number:

KEYWORDS

1. True Crime 2. Memoir  3.  Secrets

Creative direction by Nuance Art, LLC

Cover design by Temper Tantrum Tina

Editor: Chase Bolling, Alan Nixon

Werkthatart.com

Printed in United States

*For my Family*

# Introduction

Isn't it interesting? An entire line of work, hidden behind hotel doors and bathed in red light. For most, the term "sex sells" is familiar to the point of being cliché, a simple fact. But I can tell you with absolute certainty that few people understand it as well as I do. Let me explain. When a service is required, and when you can afford it, you seek out a specialist. If you want the very best clothes, you don't go to the mall. You hire a designer. If you want a house in Calabasas, you'll need a realtor at your beck and call. The supply, demand, and transaction of it all are simple. But who do you go to when you're looking for something a bit more lascivious? If you happened to be one of the richest men in the world a few decades ago, you very well might've had my number on speed dial.

*Imagine it.* All of them calling little old me, day in and day out, willing to pay whatever it would take to have their fill. But there is no such thing. So often, they grew hungrier and hungrier.

I know a lot of people have wondered what someone like myself has seen after years in the business of adult services and entertainment. But I would bet on it that some of you have curiosities that go deeper than just simple speculation. We see, every day, the rich and the famous flaunting their wealth in the obvious ways; designer clothes, expensive meals, and exclusive events are just what they allow you to see. But they have fantasies, just like you do. Things that come with a cost greater than you could imagine, but I know because I named the price and supplied the means to satisfaction. That responsibility was the defining task of my oft-maligned but incredibly in-demand former profession.

My day-to-day was not so unlike your own. My life was simple, domestic, and looked very normal to the people around me. I venture that one day, I'll talk about it all in more detail; I'll reveal how a little girl from Scotland, essentially fatherless and kept in the dark, ran away to New York and started an escort service. A story I've waited a lifetime to tell. One day.

The reality was I ran a company, not unlike so many others. I started my day at six a.m. by feeding my beloved pets, my pot-bellied pigs, and my dogs. I got breakfast ready and the table set for my four children, who were awoken with a short *tap tap* on the doors as they got up and ready for school. I made their lunches while they ate in sleepy silence, their hair still a bit tussled even though I tried to tame it for them. They were all on the bus just a little while later, never seeing mommy sit down at her desk promptly at nine a.m. to open the phone lines and respond to emails. It was a well-oiled machine; I had two bookers who handled most calls once my children were home from school and on weekends. I was on call 24/7, 365 days a year, however, to one clientele group so exclusive, they never went through my bookers: my million and billionaires. There were plenty of Forbes richest in that group, let me tell you, and I simply didn't trust anyone but myself to book for them. The stakes were simply too high. No room for mistakes in my business, that was my standard.

So, yes, a lot of what I did wasn't exactly pretty. You must understand, though, that there were times when something so unbelievably peculiar happened that there wasn't much else one could do except laugh. The requests we received in the industry, spoken with commendable confidence, would knock me out of my seat if it hadn't happened just about every time I took a call. I know these days, with all the wild things people put on the internet, some may not be so shocked as to what goes on behind closed doors.

Nevertheless, the stories I have amassed not only happened in real life; they involved some of the most influential and wealthy men on earth. Surely, you know some of their names. Others are so good at hiding, you may have never heard of them at all. Either way, their names are not so important, and their fantasies are not unlike those of our fathers, husbands, or sons. It's possible they're not so different from your own wet dreams. Their pockets are just a bit deeper, and my girls' services definitely came with a hefty price tag. That's why I am the world's most notorious madam, after all!

And with notoriety comes experience. I have gathered here some of the craziest stories from my twenty-five years as a madam. I worked hard to represent the girls I worked for with respect and loyalty. Yes, make no mistake that *I worked for them*, day and night. Thus, I was rewarded with their trust and with their tales; names, dates, and some details have been changed to protect those who deserve protecting. I hope to share with you my anecdotes of the men who kept us on our toes and certainly kept our pockets well-lined. Their desires ranged from the whimsical to the alarmingly carnal. Many were a treasure to work with. Only a handful made life a bit more difficult than it needed to be. And let's not forget that some of the girls could be a bit naughty themselves!

There are thousands of encounters to recall so I couldn't possibly tell you everything I've seen and heard (and smelled). So, here we have the odd-balls, freaks, and unpredictable turns that stood out to even the seasoned working girl. The wildest role-play that kept judges sane, surgeons steady, and athletes focused. Fantasies helped these men escape the lives they lived, release all that pent-up need for someone else to take control. Perhaps some of the happy endings my girls provided helped the millionaires become billionaires. Is that what they mean by trickledown economics?

Anyway, allow me to introduce you to the gents. You'll have a ball getting to know them. Perhaps, as you journey along, you'll get to wondering what you might do not only with all that money, but the ironclad discretion that a madam provides. I promise I won't reveal *too* much.

# Pigs in a Blanket

I was fortunate enough to have clients who were my regulars for years on end. I could predict their needs and the working relationship between us was professional, with rather defined boundaries. There was one john, though, who became a part of my everyday life in a way that felt nearly intrusive. He was such a complicated character, someone who I had a love/hate relationship with because of our unlikely codependency. To this day, I haven't been able to quite figure him out.

I have a wonderful friend in a woman named Vera. She's a proper British lady and you could trust her with the Queen's secrets. We've known each other for nearly three decades and for a long time, we worked together. She was stationed in London while I was in New York, each of us running our businesses independently but sort of "sharing" clients who moved between Europe and the States. Vera called me one day and told me of her best client who pays well and had been living in London but was planning on relocating.

"He's always been a bit eccentric, but he's just a doll underneath it all," she told me.

"And he's moving to New York permanently?" I asked. Plenty of my clients traveled a lot, but a client who'd be dividing his time between the States and England could make things complicated. What if he wanted one of my girls while he was in London? I would never step on Vera's toes just to make a buck.

"Yes, completely full-time. I imagine he'll come across the pond occasionally, but I would want you to be his contact even then. He's one hundred percent yours, darling. You know I'm plenty busy here," she insisted.

Because of his move she couldn't keep him, but she'd be happy if I would take him on. It was a call that was welcome in every sense of the word. A trusted friend, a well-paying john. What could possibly go wrong? So, he could be a tad overzealous; not a problem at all in my mind, being the motivated person that I am. I was determined to take his first night as my client and make it a massive success. All I had to do was apply my regular method!

Matching individuals is easy when you truly watch and listen to what a man is looking for. I took my time in finding him a memorable match. Mr. Strange, as I would come to call him, had a few requests that were slightly out of the ordinary, though. He told me that he was looking for a woman that was on the heavier side, unshaven (all over), and had huge breasts. Let me be clear. He wanted someone with huge, natural knockers that only a custom-fitted bra could contain. Oh, and he didn't want some young thing. She needed to be older, more mature.

The problem was that industry girls didn't usually fit this description, so I had to think outside the box. I called my C-level girls, but still, they did not please him. He let them stay an hour or so before he'd send them on their way. It got to be so frustrating that I thought I'd lose him as a client simply because I could not for the life of me find a working girl he liked, even though I was trying harder than I'd ever tried before to find the perfect match.

"Was she too young, still? Perhaps you'd be more interested in a woman around fifty or so," I suggested after another unsuccessful date.

"No, the age was fine. In fact, stick with that age, that's the sweet spot. It was something else," he claimed.

"Something else about her looks?"

"I feel like I've explained it a million times, Anna. I'm not sure how I could be any clearer. Vera never had an issue."

Thank God he couldn't see me cock my jaw at that little dig. We'd been on the phone fifteen minutes, and I had gotten nowhere with him. It was as if his ideal woman was hiding beneath a clear, plastic tarp that had been layered over her. I could see she was human, I could see her outline, but I just couldn't make out her details that would allow me to say "Ah, yes, I know who you are."

Turning to the other girls on my team, I asked if any of them had friends in other professions that were looking to make cash in a new way. Mr. Strange wanted the homely type, so I wasn't exactly finding what I was looking for in the clubs.

Finally, I got lucky with a chubby redheaded woman with pasty white skin of Irish descent. She was only about 5'4" and was well-endowed in the bust area. Perfect for Mr. Strange! I didn't have a single other client I could book her with, but it didn't matter as long as Mr. Strange took a liking to her. So, I sent her to meet him. I'd never heard him so eager to start a date after I had told him about her.

"Could she come earlier? I think you've hit the nail on the head with this one," he said excitedly, practically squealing into the phone. I held it slightly away from my ear as he spoke.

"I'm terribly sorry sir, but she's taking the train to you. I'm not sure she'll be able to make an earlier departure."

"It couldn't hurt to ask, could it? It's okay if she can't, but just check for me. I'll make it up to her, of course."

"I'll call and ask. Stay on the line," I said and put him on hold before dialing the redhead's number.

"Hi hon, how are you?"

"I'm getting ready for tonight!" She was clearly a bit anxious for her first date with a john. "Oh, God, did he cancel? I knew this would happen," she said.

"No, no! Quite the opposite. He was wondering if you could come early, now if you're available?"

"Uhm, yeah, I can. But I still have to finish my makeup, so I'll leave in a few minutes. I think I can make the next train."

"Great! I'll let him know. He should compensate you for the earlier time, so make sure he does."

"Wow, I won't even be that early. Are you sure that's necessary?"

"Sweetheart, every minute of your time is expensive," I said before exchanging goodbyes. I made Mr. Strange aware of her willingness to make it a bit early and that only made him even more eager. She made it to him about thirty minutes sooner than was previously scheduled.

They spent their time together in sweet secrecy. He had experience with so many women, all of them offering something unique. He had to ease the redhead into the murky waters of sex work, allowing her to explore him in the same ways that he was exploring her. He loved the rose gold tint of her body hair, only visible when the lamplight hit it, and ran his fingers through it with nails meeting the skin with a tense pull. She shrunk from him a little, but the thrill of the action being tied to her payment made her melt into his palm as her vulva lips parted.

He was clearly having a good time with the redhead from what I was hearing. She even spent the night a few times, which is always a sign of good things to come. I felt more confident when it came to looking for new matches, so when he asked me if I had anyone else with the redhead's heavier form, I had a much better idea of the type of woman I was looking for. That fact didn't exactly make the search easier, though! Girls who want to work in the industry *and* who looked like her are few and far between.

Things started out on the milder side with Mr. Strange for a while. He and the redhead just had some sensual alone time and watched a few movies. The few other girls I had success matching him with early on had nothing but a good time! He was a pretty good-looking man, and he was not shy when it came to compensation. When it came time again to find someone new, I spent a whole day calling around, which led me to one of my steady girl's roommates who was looking to make some extra cash. She was brunette, around 5'8", and had braces, though she was around twenty-four or twenty-five years old. I texted Mr. Strange about the possible match, prompting him to ask if she could possibly come to see him in an hour. I had her on the phone whilst I texted him.

"I could technically make it in an hour, but I feel like I should go home first. You know, freshen up, put some makeup on," she said with a lilting voice.

"Sure, I bet he wouldn't mind waiting a little bit. I'm asking him now," I said as I typed. He answered promptly. "Oh wait, he'd actually prefer you don't wear makeup. He also said not to shower."

"Really? Is he sure, cuz I'll be quick!"

"He says he's sure. As long as you're comfortable with that, I think it'd be his preference."

"Yeah, that's fine by me. Tell him I'll be there soon, then!"

"Great, I'll tell him. You two will be meeting for drinks at the Empire. Just call me again when you get there," I told her, then said goodbye.

He texted me when she arrived right away and liked this new girl very much. This is how things went on for many years; he'd want a new girl that wasn't exactly conventionally attractive, and the girls were always happy to go out with him. He was a gentleman, very kind to the girls, and handsome. I certainly didn't expect things to take a turn.

Over time, things progressively got a little weirder. He began expressing his desire for girls who would dominate him in very aggressive ways. The looks of the women he wanted to dominate him varied, but some of his favorite methods included smothering, choking, and pegging. It became a little harder to match him because not many women were comfortable enough to do what he wanted, and he wasn't usually looking for a dedicated dominatrix. He also had new requests all the time. One week he was looking for someone 200 pounds or more; the next he'd be asking for a mousey librarian type. I was going into the city two or three times a week interviewing women just for Mr. Strange. I couldn't imagine doing the same thing today; the city has changed so much, and it was intense even back then. I never truly became a city girl, I suppose, and going there that often meant that I was basically working full time for this man! Meanwhile, the girls I hired for him couldn't even get any more work with me once he was bored with them. I had to use burner phones just for speaking with his bookings to avoid the inevitable calls asking for more work. It was rough because they were all so genuinely sweet. I felt terrible that I couldn't match them with anyone else most of the time.

The years kept rolling by and Mr. Strange would come and go in unpredictable spurts. He would drive me nuts when he would pop up out of the woodwork, demanding I find him someone immediately when it used to take me weeks to find him a suitable match. I was great at my job, but I wasn't a miracle-worker! The economy had me stressed out trying to keep him as a client to pay my own piling-up bills.

He had become so difficult to please; my one super-power,

predicting the needs of men, was totally annihilated by Mr. Strange. He'd bounce from dinner and drinks with a model-type, to getting manhandled by women built like Amazons, to public stunts on London Bridge. I simply couldn't keep up.

It all came to a head when he made a request for a curvy, tall, all-American type woman at least 28 years old. I put the ad up on Craigslist and got a hit from a total Molly Ringwald lookalike, except a bit heavier. She was difficult to get a read on during the interview, coming off so carefree it was like she was in her own world. I set the date, anyway, figuring he could always send her away without much fuss.

Evidently, he liked her because he asked her to stay the night during that first meet-up. Amazingly, she declined.

"She's refusing to stay the night, Anna. I don't understand why." Mr. Strange had called to complain to me.

"Is she still there?" I asked.

"Yes, she's in the other room."

"Put her on for me. I'll see if there's something we can arrange," I told him and waited for him to give her the phone.

"Yeah?" she said, sounding irritated.

"Molly, I understand you don't want to stay overnight, is that right?"

"I just don't feel like it. I like to sleep in my own bed."

"You could always up your fee for the extra time, I know he's good for it. He really seems to like you!"

"I don't care about that. I'll stay for the time I agreed to," she said.

"Alright. Let me speak to him again."

"Hello? Did you change her mind?" Mr. Strange asked optimistically. I suppose he had walked away to give the girl her privacy while she spoke to me.

"I'm sorry, sir, but she won't be staying the night."

"Can't you make her?"

"I absolutely cannot. Please don't ask her again," I said, ending the conversation. I supported her decision, even though it meant declining several months' rent simply to sleep at home. It was always my policy that a girl could leave at their own discretion, for any reason at all. Off she went, leaving Strange confused and longing for her.

At the crack of dawn the next day, as soon as my phone lines opened up, he called demanding to see her again at 8:00 o'clock that night for dinner and a Rangers game. He also hoped she would elect to spend the night this time around. I reminded him how adamantly she refused last night, but he insisted I call and ask. She agreed to dinner and the game, but it was another hard no for the sleepover. In fact, she wanted to be home by ten for a good night's sleep. I'd never met a girl with such squeaky-clean sleep hygiene. They went on for weeks like that, him always begging her to spend the night and her stubbornly refusing to do so. It became an obsession for him to try and sway her, to no avail.

He suddenly disappeared for about six months. In the meantime, I finally got a much-needed break from the toll his demands were taking on me. My pocketbook was a bit lighter for it, but we all make sacrifices for our mental fortitude. When he reappeared, he was right back to asking for Molly Ringwald. She was the only girl he would even consider, simply refusing to see anybody but her. I'm not sure why she continued to agree to see him, but she did go out with him that night, which included an unexpected twist.

He called to inform me that he would be leaving an envelope under his door with a code word and a room key. Molly understood the instructions perfectly, though I was utterly out of the loop. She arrived as directed, let herself in, and discovered a myriad of toys for her to choose from. There were two sets of handcuffs, a ball gag, a blindfold, and a code word indicating which character she'd be playing that night. Apparently, this little scene was something they'd been discussing privately. She'd be acting as the pissed, bitchy ex-girlfriend that night, throwing out mean insults and handcuffing Mr. Strange to the bed so he'd just have to lay there and take it. She either got bored or hungry because she ordered thirteen pigs in a blanket and bought a pay-per-view movie. Mr. Strange was totally ignored for about forty-five minutes before she up and left him still handcuffed to the bed. His grunts of protest went unanswered as Molly waltzed her way out of the room back to her home. Hotel staff discovered him that evening when they arrived for the scheduled turn-down service.

He called me absolutely furious with how the evening had transpired.

"I was completely humiliated! The whole world could've found out about this if the staff had recognized me, thank God that they didn't!" He was ranting nonstop for many minutes about how this incident could've destroyed his reputation and I completely understood his rage.

"Trust me, this will not happen again. And you won't be paying a cent for it, I assure you," I said since I had no other choice than to give him the night free and absorb Molly's fee.

"You're damn right I won't be paying for that nightmare. We had an agreement, and she broke it," he said, sounding a bit dejected about this whole situation beneath all that anger.

I couldn't believe what she said when I called her demanding a reason for her behavior

"He just looked so pathetic, like one of those pigs in a blanket. He's childish and annoying and I was sick of looking at him, so I left."

"That's hardly a reason to leave a client in such a compromised position. I'm afraid to book you with him again, let alone a new client who might be interested down the line!"

"I promise it wouldn't happen with anyone else. I just don't think I can go out with him anymore," she said nonchalantly.

9

"Well, we'll see what happens. I'll let you know if I hear from anyone else," I said then hung up with her. Mr. Strange vanished once again, and I figured I would never hear from him again.

You know how this goes by now, right? He resurfaced just a few months later like a persistent zit and demanded Molly. Only this time, she refused to even see him again. There wasn't enough money in the world to change her mind. She offered to go see anybody but him. She was through with her little piggy. She claimed he was childish and boring. I could see where she was coming from. The psycho was sending me fifty or sixty texts a day in an attempt to get Molly back. All I could do was ask her, especially when he offered to triple the price he would pay just to see her again. I suppose his desperation piqued her interest because she gave him a counteroffer. All he had to do was give his credit card number to a little boutique space called Pandora's Box in the city so she could do a little shopping. Some latex bodysuits and paddles surely would mend their strained relationship. This gesture was the only way he could make things up to her. He did not hesitate to do as she asked, and she was happy to spend $9,000 curtesy of her little piggy. Such a price tag sent me into hidden hysterics. Mr. Strange, true to his name, was unfazed and mostly relieved that he'd be allowed to see her again. She went to him with her new gear in tow, finally electing to stay the night. Maybe I was a miracle-worker, after all! He called the following week, at the worst possible time might I add, and I confidently asked if he'd like me to reach out to Molly. "No," he replied. "Who's new?" I was slack jawed as my kids and their friends sang loudly to the radio as I drove them to a track meet. I quickly regained my composure, speaking in what could only be called code to placate and book Mr. Strange while keeping the kids out of the loop. When I had finally passed him off to finish the call with my booker, I didn't really know what to think. I was just grateful that amid all the chaos that this client brought into my life, the only thing the kids were paying attention to was Lady Gaga on the radio.

Thus, the pig in the blanket affair came to an abrupt close. Not to worry, though. Mr. Strange remained a constant necessary perturbance in my life.

# Pin Man

The interesting thing about being a madam, besides how wild it is to even hold such a title, is how unique some people are when it comes to their kinks. There seemed an infinite way to indulge in all your typical categories; you could be into domination, but it could be verbal or physical, painful, or sexy. The possibilities were truly endless. I found myself wondering how they developed an idea that would never occur to most people. One man that comes to mind was named Bert. He was the chairman of one of the biggest investment banking firms in the world. When he wasn't making ginormous financial decisions involving sums of money none of us could ever dream of, he was booking a domme through my services, about once every three or four weeks.

Again, it was a sexless arrangement that Bert was looking for as he had dommes come by his Park Avenue apartment for some good, old-fashioned domination and humiliation. What I've mentioned already in other stories is nothing compared to the full spectrum of what dommes have seen and done for their clients. When I first spoke to Bert, I didn't expect him to be the "type". He was less jittery than other subs were on the phone, and this

Harvard-educated man really was one of the last true gentlemen I'd ever encountered. However, as we booked him more and we spoke more often, I realized that Bert had tastes that were far off the beaten path.

He'd been booking with us for a little while when he asked if I had anyone new I could pair him with. As a matter of fact, I certainly did. I had been holding off on pairing him with my top domme, Jaz, until he had a reliable track record with my lower rankings. Jaz was the best you could get when it came to dominatrices; she was a tall, curvy redhead with a headstrong personality. She wouldn't take shit from anyone, and even I knew not to mess with her. She wasn't mean or aggressive; she just really embodied what it meant to be a domme at that time. Maybe things have changed now, but either way, she was the kind of tough bitch that subs couldn't get enough of. I gave her the time and address to meet Bert and she said she'd be there, already seeing dollar signs after hearing the location. Interestingly, I already had a few clients living on Park Avenue, one even in the same building Bert lived in.

She arrived at Bert's mansion-sized apartment unsure of what his particular kink would turn out to be. It could be anything from spanking to getting tied up and yelled at. She'd seen it all, so she thought. She wasn't worried. Bert welcomed her in, clearly having dismissed his home staff hours earlier. He offered her a drink, but she asked for just a cranberry seltzer, wanting to keep her wits about her until she knew what to expect with this new guy. They made small talk for only a few minutes before he asked if she'd follow him to another wing of his place. This area was private, he mentioned. The marble flooring and high ceilings of the hallway were stunning and bright, a stark contrast to the room they entered at the end of it.

The room was reminiscent of a ritzy home office but much larger and darker. Lining the walls were display hooks burdened with bondage toys and straps, though there were familiar elements like a large mahogany desk, leather sofa, and bookshelves. Sitting on the desk, almost innocently, was a locked wooden box. Bert unlocked it when they entered but did not mention it, nor did he open it to reveal its contents. That would come a little later. In the middle of the room, a massage table was beckoning to the pair, but Bert led Jaz to the sofa first, so he could explain what the next two hours held in store for her. He wasted no time with pleasantries and got right into it.

"I like to be tied up, so tight I can't escape. All day long, I'm ordering people around, and sometimes, I'm ruining the lives of people who've never done anything wrong to deserve it. I need to be punished for all the pain I'm causing," he said, eyes desperate. Jaz nodded, a sly smile spreading across her face. She was so damned curious about what was in the box, and she hoped her patience would be rewarding.

Bert removed his bathrobe and lay down on the massage table. Jaz took leather straps and fastened them over his slightly bulging belly, arms, and legs. Then, she blindfolded him. Finally, he asked her to bring the box over. She did so, and what she found inside was not at all what she had expected.

She thought the box might contain a script or maybe nipple clamps, something she'd seen before. Instead, within the little box were two black felt pincushions, but you almost couldn't even see them because they were covered in shiny, thin, two-inch silver pins. She was confused for a moment, thinking *what the fuck are these for*, but she got the gist after a second of thought. Now, she had the missing piece to the puzzle, and they could begin.

Bert was a bloodsucking businessman, and, for that, he thought the only equal punishment was to let some blood himself, an attempt to make things even. This was all about pain and release, almost like a confessional. He would atone for his sins, one way or another. Drawing blood wasn't usually on the menu for Jaz, however, and she was having second thoughts, which she voiced.

"Are you sure about this?" she asked.

"I'll double the payment. Just make me bleed, Mistress. I deserve it," Bert assured her. Nothing more needed to be said after that and, even though it made Jaz a little squeamish, she was happy to do it for such great compensation. Everyone has a price, I suppose.

She took the first pin and poked him with it, but it wasn't enough. Bert wanted the pins to stay in him, so Jaz had to push till she broke the skin. She started with his arms, and he didn't flinch much from that, even though he was accumulating them quickly and all were in him nearly a quarter inch deep. She covered him with them, a hundred or more of them until he made one last request: stick his testicles. It took a few seconds of mustering up the courage, but she did what she was asked to, sticking five pins in each ball. He looked rather horrifying, laying there as a human pincushion. After the last pin was in him, Bert was hard and ready for his release. Jaz took a cane from the wall, one that had feathers on the end. She tickled him all over, his demented laugh-grunting echoing off the walls when she tickled at his erection.

"Untie my hand!" he begged. Once it was loose, he shifted slightly away from Jaz and came onto the floor. His self-inflicted punishment had drawn to a close and Jaz undid the rest of his restraints, but he was still covered in pins!

"Do you want me to help get all those out?" she asked, astonished that he was just walking around like that.

"Not at all," he said, his back facing her as he walked to his desk. He pulled a thick wad of cash from a drawer and brought it to her. It was much more than the doubled fee he had mentioned, but Jaz certainly wasn't complaining. She showed herself out after wishing him a very good rest of his night. Bert took no pleasure in his work and therefore could not enjoy his play without pain. It was the familiar sensation, the hair-raising, prickly sensation he experienced every time he forced somebody's hand in their dealings. Jazz didn't need to know all the details to get the gist; he thought he deserved what she did to him and perhaps he was right. Such is the life of a professional dominatrix, doling out consequences for guilty consciences.

# Rockstar Ron

Some regulars were *very* regular. Regular clients, booking once a month or more, made up most of my client base. Others were consistent for years and years, but I didn't have the pleasure of serving them very often. I had a gent who was not as well off as most of my other clients, but one would not dare consider him middle-class. He was still a very wealthy man and was able to pay for his parents' medical expenses, nursing homes, and the like, as they grew older. He had sadly lost his wife and had no children. His wife, Maria, was his high school sweetheart, and he married her as soon as his business started. She had been his true love; he spoke of her often and always in the present tense as if she was still waiting for him at their home. He owned a sort of mom-and-pop type company that required him to work insanely long hours, year-round. Every year, around mid-May, I'd get a call so we could begin planning his big June fourth birthday bash.

His name was Ron, likely one of my favorite clients to plan for. If you saw him on the street, you would never suspect the desires of this sweet, older gentleman. He reminded me of a man I had met during my childhood while I was still living in Scotland. I was running around with a few other girls at the time and frequented a small bakery in the afternoons, just before close. He was always gracious with us, even though we were rowdy and unkempt. His sandy grey hair fell over his brow, offsetting the redness of his cheeks and nose. Ron was similarly cheerful and hardworking. All he wanted was to be treated, for just one night, as the most important person in the room. What with the era he grew up in, he positively idolized the Rolling Stones and other high caliber rockstars. Everything about that lifestyle was a fantasy to him. The man knew what his reality was, of course, spending long hours taking care of others who depended on him. It was especially meaningful to me and my girls that Ron was well taken care of with a party he would never forget. The only other thing he had to look forward to otherwise was the kind gesture of a cake from his staff.

There wasn't a detail I let slip through the cracks. Typically, I'd begin by hiring a car service to pick Ron up in the newest luxury vehicle available, windows deeply tinted to conceal his identity. The girls were great people to go to for tips on the hottest clubs and restaurants that had VIP tables and could accommodate a large crowd. I'm sure the cake Ron's staff got him was lovely, but I always ordered from an amazing bakery on Atlantic Avenue. They also made the best blueberry pie I'd ever tried, but Ron was more interested in something tall and fabulously decorated. This leads me to the girls! Oh, the girls would fawn over him all night, squealing when they popped the champagne at his table, making everyone turn their heads to see who was celebrating in such raucous style. The girls would come bearing gifts that I had hand-picked and wrapped, though I would be reimbursed later. The final detail was the finest hotel suite for Ron and his groupies to party the rest of the night away.

It took time, to plan such an event. Ron and I would spend a while going back and forth on the phone hammering out all the intricacies and making this party even greater than last year's. He liked to choose one girl who had been at his party before, for comfort and familiarity with how the event would go. He liked tall playmate girls with blonde hair and natural busts.

When the day finally came, Ron would call me from his hotel to let me know he was settled in and ready to rock. The car and the girls would be sent his way promptly and then the party could get started! Ron would finally be the center of the universe as the girls hung on his arm through dinner and drinks. He really was a sweetie, even going so far as to bring each girl a little token of his appreciation once they arrived. It was a gesture most husbands never even think of, but not Ron. He was a charmer through and through. The girls always made around $1,000 each, plus tips. Having more money than you know what to do with doesn't always mean you're generous. Plenty of my billionaires were a little stingy, but Ron went beyond generosity, and he wasn't even as rich as some! He deserved every ounce of attention he got during his birthday celebrations; his demeanor was what made him one of our VIP's, even if he didn't have the highest budget.

Champagne on ice got things going in the car, then the posse would sit down at their reserved table for a five-course meal. The cake would be delivered to the table, more than they could possibly finish. Don't tell anyone, but sometimes I had a bit of it wrapped up and brought to my apartment a few blocks away. It was way too good to let go to waste! After dessert, it was off to the club for even more special treatment. I'd make sure the club let Ron and his beauties skip the line and head straight back to the VIP section. Ron, flanked by six-foot twenty-somethings in stilettos, never walked as confidently as he did at that moment. The world was his and he had the stuff to prove it. Champagne flowed like a river for Ron and transformed this average man in his fifties into freakin' Mick Jagger. He was a sight to see. I wondered what his late wife might've thought of all this, but I felt certain that if she had still been alive, Ron would've never sought out my services. He just needed a smidgen of revelry to get him through the years without her, I think.

Ron and the girls would eventually leave the club to retire to his suite, partaking in an extra fun slumber party fit for a king. The ladies helped Ron out of his suit and led him into the grand master bathroom. The jacuzzi tub beckoned playful as bubbles spilled over the edge, filling the room with a peachy scent. They popped bottles in the tub and Ron glugged it down, wishing he had more hands. His vixens modeled for him, all the while giggling and planting kisses across his chest and cheeks, layering perfect red lip prints that faded as they got lower and lower. The tub was left behind as it got lukewarm, making the California king mattress all the more inviting for a party of five. Not one lady was left untouched or unsatisfied by Ron's sweet, giving nature. But only one was the lucky gal that got to finish him off before he drifted off to a heavenly sleep, where dreams simply couldn't compete with that night's reality. A perfect ending to a perfect birthday. I was thrilled to hear all about it from Ron the following morning when he'd give me a call and tell me about how much fun he had.

"You really outdid yourself this time, Anna! When we got to the club, the music was so loud I had to turn down my hearing aid! And these three other girls started dancing with us all out of the blue and pretty much clung to me all night. Was that another one of the tricks up your sleeve?" Ron asked, delighting in all the details.

"I wish it was! Oh, it sounds like it was a great night, hon. How was the suite?"

"Stunning, really. I mean, you know I love The St. Regis, but it was nice to try something new. I'd never stayed at, uh…what was it called again?"

"The Mark," I said, thinking about all the sweettalking it took to book that reservation.

"Yeah, The Mark! Oh my gosh, it was like we weren't even in the city anymore. It felt like Paris or something."

"Well, it's my pleasure. You keep in touch, okay?" I said, knowing I probably wouldn't hear from him for many, many months.

He would always rave about how it was the best birthday so far. I'm sure he would've said as much even if it wasn't true, but I believed he was being honest. Next year, we'd do it all over again.

You see, I was so much more than just a madam. I was an event planner, a travel agent, and oftentimes a friend to those who needed a bit of fun in their otherwise taxing lives. Since my first days in the business, I would always ask a gent's birthday if he came around a second time. It was a half-off special that really meant a lot to the regulars. A small detail that enabled me to make lasting connections, create a safe environment, and always resulted in a delighted customer.

# Mr. Bond, the Valtrex Man

The greatest thing someone in my industry could find was a girl everyone loved. I had a steady girl who had seen just about all of my client base several times. The only trouble was clients like to see a new face and this girl wasn't getting the amount of work she used to. I wanted to keep getting her clients, so I put a new ad up online, detailing a "fitness and swimwear magazine model seeking benefactor". The ad blew up and after screening a handful of potential clients, we followed up with a prospective gentleman we got to know as James Bond. He was a colorful character if there ever was one.

He had a rather specific idea for his first date with the fitness model. Not unusual in the industry, although he was more confident in sharing his bizarre fantasy than I expected he would be since he was pretty normal sounding on the phone. People will never surprise you more than when they entrust you with their secrets. I always tried to look at new clients as a blank slate and reflect on how first impressions are rarely a good guide as to how a man will behave in the future. It's just a crapshoot, really.

He requested that she wear thigh-high leather boots with

heels, a short skirt, a ponytail, glasses, and have a plastic handgun with her. When he arrived at my discreet apartment location, where so many scenes of roleplay and make-believe played out, she must greet him with, "Hello Mr. Bond. May I take your briefcase?" He also gave me a role-play script, which I passed on to my girl after reading it myself. Unfazed, she agreed to meet him.

He arrived on time and greeted her with, "I have the documents."

"May I see them now?" she replied. At this point, Bond was anxiously searching around the room for anybody hidden from his view. He demanded she lower the shades over the windows. Suddenly, the girl lunged for the briefcase, causing her and Mr. Bond to tumble to the floor in a frenzy, each one tugging at the bag.

"Mr. Bond, I need those documents now!"

"Then give me the code so I can deliver them," he shouted.

"Code? I need no code. I'm taking these documents with or without your consent," she demanded, pulling the plastic gun from her hip. "Strip, asshole. You're not gonna get away with this."

He complied, a scowl just barely disguising the pleased look in his eyes. He had little scars on his chest around his nipples that looked like he'd been pinched with those black document clips over and over, long ago. Once he was standing there, shaking in his boxers, she slapped him open-handed across the face. He removed his last article of clothing in a hurry. She cupped his balls in her hand, and it was cold. She fondled him only for a second or two before grabbing and twisting, causing him to fall to his knees with a breathless pant.

She roughed him up while he lay defenseless on the ground. He pleaded for mercy, promising he wouldn't tell anyone about the documents if she would just let him go and not assassinate him. All this time, his erection grew. I recall the girl mentioning he even got out a little crocodile tear in the midst of being slapped around. Good actor, I suppose.

The scene ended with her high-heeled boot pressing into his chest while she said "Mr. Bond, you are under my control. I order you to finish while I watch. If you do, I'll let you have your precious documents back." He self-gratified as her heel dug into his sternum, finishing once it broke the skin just enough to bleed. All the while, the case they'd been fighting over, the "documents", actually contained her fee. She left the apartment with the case swinging in her hand, Mr. Bond watching and spreading his seed across his bare stomach.

Some time passed before we heard from Mr. Bond again, though the mission was a success. He did call eventually, though, with hopes for us to arrange another scene, this time with a girl of exceptional athletic abilities. He wanted her to have some knowledge of kickboxing or MMA. This time around, the role-play was a winner-takes-all cage match, so our lady boxer would need to come in an Everlast sports bra, spandex shorts, hair tied up, boxing gloves, and a mouth guard for an adult male. Mr. Bond was kind enough to offer to pay for the boxing gloves if his date didn't have her own, but he was in luck! I found a girl who was a total fitness addict, spending two or more hours in the gym every day. Of course, she had her own gloves.

When the pair met up, Mr. Bond played a CD he had burned himself of a Valtrex commercial in which two girls appear to be getting ready to box. Valtrex had an interesting string of commercials of people doing all sorts of fun activities as the narrator in the background talked about the various side effects of the drug used to treat their herpes. Commercials are like that all the time now, but back then it wasn't so overdone. He watched the commercial with an intensity she took to mean he was getting hot about it already. Then he outlined his desire.

He wanted his girl to box him until he was black, blue, and

purple. The CD played on a loop as she beat him without relent. Despite, or should I say due to, his bruising and bleeding, he paid her full fare plus a hefty tip. He even said he would be back for more! She worked up quite the sweat knocking Mr. Bond onto his butt over and over again, so much so she skipped the gym for the next two days. Meanwhile, this well-built, handsome older gentleman would have some explaining to do considering his swollen face and battered upper body. She was even concerned she had seriously done damage to him, considering his advanced age, but he was nothing but thrilled with the walloping she had given him. I really wonder what he told his employees and partners when he went to work the following day. I assume they thought he had been mugged or something along those lines; someone as highly positioned as he could certainly be a target for such a crime. "No need to press charges," he must've assured them, "just tripped over the dog last night and clipped my face on the coffee table." The assault was entirely consensual, and it was his giddy little secret for everyone to fuss over him, all the while he knew the truth of the situation.

I was lying in bed one night watching TV when a client of mine made an appearance on the news segment "Shame on You". He owned a restaurant near Rockefeller Center which had always done a lot of business. Apparently, he'd been deliberately raising the prices on the menu around Christmas time, gouging patrons in an already expensive eatery. I dozed off thinking about how he never used any of that money to tip my girls a pretty penny. I was nudged awake by my husband.

"Looks like you're going to need a much bigger apartment, honey," he smirked.

"Really? And why's that?" I asked as I noticed the new Valtrex commercial airing. It had a couple canoeing. We both cracked up at the thought of Mr. Bond's possible new fantasy.

Mr. Bond did make a new request, but I guess Valtrex was out. This time he wanted two women of African descent, dressed in "tribal wear with floral wraps and sandals." He claimed it would be the perfect setup for him to role-play as Indiana Jones running from Amazon Warriors, leading to an epic fight for the Key of Doom. He called it "the thrill of a lifetime". I called it a new low, but at least he was a big tipper.

# Beat the Clock

The phone rang, and a familiar voice with a recognizably playful tone said, "Know anyone intelligent, maybe new, who likes to play games?"

"Hmm," I replied. "I recently met a girl with her Master's in teaching a few weeks ago. She has a great imagination." I went on to describe the 5'7", all American girl with a bubbly personality. She was highly intellectual and had no tattoos or odd piercings. You might describe her as the sexy professor type. The date with gorgeous Lindsay was set for Thursday at 2:00 pm, for which she was prepped prior to arriving. Remember, the gent had requested a special game for them to play.

The gent, named John, was really into playing with a Rubik's cube. He was good, too, which is probably why he liked this game so much. The game also involved a whip and an egg timer. Lindsay waved me off as I explained. "Let him surprise me," she said. "I think I see where we're going with this."

Women in this industry really have seen and heard it all, so their predictions about a gent's kink are frequently spot on. Sure, Lindsay hadn't ever worked with a man who had this particular combination of props, but she wasn't judging. As long as everyone's needs are met and we're all consenting adults, where is the crime?

Lindsay arrived at the hotel on Thursday promptly at 1:55 pm. Company policy was that if you're not early, you're late.

John welcomed her into his room, standing before her like some Harvard professor, or at least his imaginary caricature of one. Moving a briefcase and newspaper off the chair for Lindsay to settle in, he offered her a drink, which she readily agreed to. They engaged in many minutes of worldly chitchat, discussing new motives in scientific research and the upcoming exhibitions set to take place at the Met. Then John asked, "Do you like playing games?"

"Yes, of course," Lindsay replied. "Especially difficult ones."

"Perfect," John smiled as he took from his briefcase the Rubik's cube, egg timer, and a short English riding crop. Now the game could begin.

Lindsay set the timer for three minutes and shouted "yellow!" He worked frantically, rolling the cube over and over in his hands until the yellow side was totally complete with only a moment to spare. He laughed and told Lindsay to remove her blouse, such were the rules. She did so, then set the timer for another three minutes. It was the white side he had to complete this time, but the timer went off before he could. Only two squares away, the bastard! He got two lashes for it, Lindsay spanking him on his thigh with the crop.

John turned a little red in the face and shook his head. "I'll get it this time, Professor," he promised. Red was next and John was working desperately to solve the puzzle. He did it just as the timer buzzed! Now Lindsay was to remove her skirt. The game went back and forth like that for about half an hour or more, ending when either Lindsay was fully disrobed, or John failed multiple times in a row to complete a side. This time, the game ended with the latter. John was bent over on the bed, khakis around his argyled ankles, so Lindsay could give his butt a good spanking with the crop. He wasn't a total glutton; she spanked him just hard enough to hear the snap of the leather and redden his cheeks (both sets).

"Please, Professor, let me try one more time! I'll get it right," John begged as Lindsay snapped at his bare bottom, pausing briefly to reply.

"Fine, one more chance. If you fail again, however, you will not be allowed to receive your reward."

It all came down to this. John, pants still down, sat on the chair and picked the Rubik's cube up once more. Lindsay set the timer and he was off like a madman to solve the blue side, moving his fingers fast as lightning. He completed it with the biggest grin on his face.

"What a smart boy you are! I believe you have earned your reward. Go ahead, I'll watch the clock," Lindsay said, picking the timer up to set it for the last time of the afternoon. All she had to do now was sit back and watch him finish himself off. He never needed all ninety seconds for this final puzzle. He could do this one with his eyes closed.

I'm not quite sure where he came up with this little game, but I thought it was cute. Harmless and sexless, the girls were always tipped well and left happily. Many a dominatrix would be overjoyed to have a session as easy as it was with John.

# The Rabbi's Blessing

B en was a good friend and consistent client for over a decade. As a john, he was easygoing but odd in his mannerisms. He was approximately 5'4", around 60 years old when he first started using my service, with long payos and beard. He was, and still is, a prominent rabbi in the Brooklyn Hasidic community. He acted as a sort of judge and member of a panel, to my understanding.

Inside and outside of our working relationship, this was a reserved man. His clothing was modest and clearly dated. He had a very basic taste in women. He liked ladies who were blonde, natural, and without implants or heavy makeup. His biggest turnoff was anyone who was heavily scented, pleasantly or otherwise. He refused smokers or girls who wore any type of perfume. He just had a preference for the simple things, I suppose. He, unlike most of my clients, would latch onto a certain girl to create a more familiar relationship with them. He liked that kind of closer bond so he could feel a bit more comfortable. One such lady was named Jenny. Unfortunately for Ben, she was the sweetest, prettiest thing, but notoriously late for every date I sent her on. I had tried, on many occasions, to purposefully tell her the date was two hours earlier than it was scheduled for, but it didn't matter. Somehow, she would still be late. Maybe she had caught on to my ruse! Either way, it sent Ben into a tizzy every time she kept him waiting, making him even more desperate for her. He was like a lost puppy, wandering around the block no matter the weather and calling me every few minutes to ask if Jenny would arrive soon. He was never angry with her, only disappointed and worried she had begun to dislike him. That was absolutely not the case, however. The girls who historically dated Ben were completely endeared to him. He was so sweet, they would tell me. Jenny was just too easily distracted to be reliable. Still, she was a good girl to have around, and Ben would have been devastated if I let her go.

Ben's usual appointment, be that with Jenny or another girl he liked, would begin with him calling ahead so I could have a cleaning lady come into the apartment before he and his lady friend arrived. He was a total germaphobe, so the place had to be scrubbed from top to bottom with bleach. I think that was the only scent he enjoyed, in fact.

Once Jenny finally arrived at the apartment, Ben was told he could head up and begin. She greeted him at the door wearing a conservative blouse and skirt, devoid of any stains or imperfections. She had prepared the apartment with a box of tissues available on the table and a fresh set of sheets in a plastic bag labeled "Ben" set on the sofa. Ben entered, checking the kitchen and closets then looking out the window to ensure no one could see him.

"Looks like the coast is clear, Ben. Can I get you anything?" Jenny asked, her hands clasped behind her bottom as she swayed.

"You never know who might be watching," Ben said, subconsciously raising his hand to the top of his head. "A ginger ale would help calm me, I believe."

Jenny knew the routine. She took an already clean glass from the cabinet and washed it in the small kitchen sink, minding the water as steam wafted from the basin. She thoroughly dried it with a paper towel before pouring the can of ginger ale into the now warm glass. "You're right, this'll help if you sip it," she said.

"You're too kind, Jenny, too good to me. Sit with me, yes?"

Ben laid the sheets overtop the sofa and the leather chair that was adjacent to it. The first hour and a half of the date consisted of just talking together on the sofa, discussing Jenny's life and dreams.

"So, tell me," he began, "how is life treating you?"

"Everything is good, pretty much the same as always. But I'm thinking maybe I want to go back to school."

"An education is so important, zissele. So lucrative for a girl to have beauty and brains. To what end?"

"Maybe I could be a teacher in the future. I love kids, and I think it would be good for me."

"Oi, you are a saint. Teaching the young ones, how lovely that sounds. But college can be difficult. You must prepare yourself for those hard times that God might challenge you with. But you are already so strong and resourceful, I have no worries about your success," Ben said with a sincere shimmer in his eyes.

The pair didn't touch at all during the conversation, but it was intimate, nonetheless. Ben maintained eye contact and nodded as Jenny did her best to be honest with the man without revealing that this was all just a part of her job. She struggled to remember what she had told him in the past to keep up the lie she was stringing along. She ought to have kept a notebook on it with how often she and Ben spoke.

After a while, however long it took for him to work up the courage that time around, he'd ask Jenny if it would be okay to touch her. "Yes, of course," she'd reply. That was her queue to remove her blouse, revealing a sexy lace bra concealing her pert breasts. Ben averted his gaze, just barely taking one second peeks at Jenny's body. His face flushed bright red. She scooted closer to him, thinking about how cute it was that he got so embarrassed. She wondered if he had been handsome as a young man. Maybe not handsome, but sweet and probably not entirely ugly. She wondered if they would've been friends. They might've been, and then she could've been more honest with him than she could be now.

"You're the most beautiful woman I've ever seen," Ben stuttered. He grazed the lace of Jenny's bra with his fingertips, unable to physically grasp her in any serious way. He moved to the leather seat at that time, requesting Jenny remove her skirt so he could better look at her legs and the pretty pinkness that lay between them. With her heels still on, Jenny gracefully modeled for Ben on the couch. He was in awe of the way she arched her back and faced him with something he had forbidden himself to touch. He cursed under his breath and rubbed sweaty hands on his thighs until he couldn't resist any longer. But what he did is not at all what you'd expect of a man who has full access to the woman in the room with him.

He'd stand up suddenly and turn his back to Jenny. He could barely get out his words as he pleaded.

"Don't move, please. Oh, God, yes. No, no, don't come closer!"

Jenny could hear him lower his zipper and begin to grunt softly. It took him no time at all to release into the tissue he had in hand, which was quickly folded and put into his pocket. As Jenny dressed, Ben washed and sanitized his hands. Then he offered one final question.

"Jenny, may I give you a blessing?"

"Of course, Rabbi. I'd be honored."

Jenny kneeled at his feet as he spoke over her a blessing in his fluent Hebrew. Once the prayer was complete, Ben turned and left. Every girl who had been booked by Ben had accepted the Rabbi's blessing. Why deny what could only be pure generosity? Not only in that form, but in the sizable tip he left for his blessed beauties.

Five minutes later, I'd get a call from Ben asking if the girl had a good time and if she'd like to continue seeing him. I'd always say, "I'm sure it was wonderful, I'll hear from her soon. She has to clean up and collect her fee first." I'd ask him to wait about thirty minutes. This was the routine, and, like a broken record, I'd assure Ben of the girls having a nice time with him and call him again thirty minutes later to confirm that fact.

# The Doctor Will See You Now

What Madam's assortment of gents would be complete without a wannabe doctor as a regular? In this case, Tom was a well-known veterinarian who specialized in orthopedic bone reconstruction surgeries. He had designed and preformed many pioneering procedures that had benefitted countless animals.

Veterinary medicine hadn't been his dream at the beginning. While in medical school, he was caught snorting cocaine and also tested positive for marijuana in his system when they forced him to undergo a drug screening. He was expelled from his program, which had been none other than gynecology. He had to find a different outlet for his medical background because no respectable med school would have him. By some miracle, he was accepted to a veterinary program outside the States, making it a bit harder for the university to track down his unsavory expulsion. Many years passed and he went on to secure a successful veterinary practice, making a respectable living. His original dream nagged at him, though, and evolved into something slightly less selfless than supporting women's health.

Tom would call us every few months to book a girl for an

exam. Yes, you read that right. I narrowed down the roster of girls for him because some refused to participate, and I didn't want him picking a girl I knew wouldn't be into it. There was still a large selection of willing women that we'd look through together before he found his perfect patient.

"Is she...generally healthy?" he'd ask as we went through the photos while online together.

"Oh, definitely. I mean, I don't know of any specifics, but her skin is just radiant, and she takes great care of herself," I replied.

"Hmm. Sounds like she doesn't need my help."

"Well, there's this girl here that might. Had to take a few weeks off a while ago to help an ailing family member. Breast cancer, I believe," I lied. I'd never give away a girl's information like that to a client. It was all about creating a story for him.

"That must've been terrible for her. God forbid she goes unscreened with such a history. I'd like to see her."

She'd arrive at his veterinary practice after hours via a car service we used. The car would wait there for her, not only to get her back home promptly but to assure her she could leave at any time without needing to wait for a ride. There's more room for danger when one of my girls was in a client's environment rather than the environment I offered. Extra precautions were always taken. Tom was not a threat in the slightest. It's just better to be safe than sorry.

When she arrived, he'd meet her at the door and lead her back to an examination room he kept locked at all other times. It was never questioned by his staff because he was the boss. What were they going to do, demand he open it? So, his secret was always safe. Within the room, there was a gynecology chair, stirrups and all, a short chair on wheels, and an overhead lamp. The countertop had a speculum and magnifying glass carefully placed on sterilized pans. When he greeted her, he'd already be dressed in his lab coat and teal scrubs. I recall sending a seasoned girl to him one time, named Cara, but she only saw him that one time. She refused to go through it again and I'm sure you'll understand why.

He began the examination with a thorough history of her sexual and medical background, so he asked, "How many sexual partners have you had, approximately?"

"I guess I'd say about ten, maybe fifteen. Over the course of many years, obviously," Cara replied, knowing the number was much higher.

"And are you always practicing safe sex?"

"Not always." Another lie. Condoms were a must for her, being that this was her full-time job.

"Hmm, interesting. When was the last time you had a menstrual cycle?"

"Three weeks ago."

"So, you should be having it soon, then."

"Yeah, I should. I'm pretty regular."

"Good, that's good. It says in your chart that your family has a history of breast cancer. You're a bit young for them, but are you preparing for that fact? I mean, not that it's certain, but you may need to consider getting a mammogram earlier than most women," he said, eying her chest.

"It's on my mind, but no, I haven't really done anything to take precautions," she replied, leaning forward and raising one eyebrow at the good doctor.

"Well, then we absolutely must do a breast exam today. I'm also going to perform a pelvic exam afterward. Who in your family has been affected by the disease?"

"Uhm…" Cara thought for a moment. How could he ask something like that? She was sure he knew a real gyno would never. And she didn't want to jinx anyone. "Both my grandmothers," she said solemnly. Both had already passed, and she figured she couldn't give the dead bad luck.

"How's about we get started. Let's take a look," he said, reaching for the bottom of her blouse. She lifted her arms as her shirt came up and over her face, then was tossed aside. He undid her bra for her. The chill in the room was having its effect on her, but Tom took it for arousal. "Left arm up," he said, taking her right breast in his hand and kneading. "Now the right. God, they feel amazing. I don't think you have any reason to worry but let me be sure." He stood to the side of the examination chair, sort of shifting her to face away from him. He put his hands all over her torso, massaging her neck and tracing his fingers across her nipples. The scent of her hair was intoxicating and made him push himself up against her exposed back.

After the intake session, Tom asked his patient to lie back while he put on his gloves, a surgical mask, and headlight.

Cara was having a hard enough time pretending to tell this guy about her made-up medical history. When he was finally done with the mental probing and outward inspection, it was time to get a bit closer. Cara didn't think this would be too difficult. She had her feet up and he began examining her. Occasionally, he'd break the silence with "Wow, you're so tight" or "you're so soft and clean." Tom used a warming lube that he thought must help the girls get in the mood, but this was Cara's third appointment that week. She was ready for a long weekend spent with her girlfriends. This exam was less arousing than seeing an actual gynecologist.

But Tom was far from finished. He had toys to use, and Cara played along convincingly. She rubbed herself with the vibrator Tom handed to her. She had to squint her eyes every time the dummy would look up at her with the silly headlamp on. It was practically blinding! Using the vibrator on herself helped a lot. She didn't need Tom to help her orgasm, even though in his mind it was all his doing. He kept his fingers in her as she finished, convinced he was this guru of sexual fantasy. He was what we girls called "a lover". He wanted to take his time and give the girl a lot of attention. It was sweet, in a weird way, but these girls are working. Their clients are not their romantic partners if you see what I mean. A lover simply takes too long for them and frequently isn't as good as they think they are. Interestingly, not a single girl complained about the men who liked to talk, like Ben. They saved their little teasing for the men that liked to spend hours in the daisy fields, frolicking endlessly. Nevertheless, everyone was satisfied, despite the pair having totally separate mental experiences. Tom really was a pleasant man, even with his secret little exam room. He sent the girl off after paying a nice fee, even giving her a few samples of the lube he used on her as a parting gift. Because that's what lovers do, of course!

# Girls Gone Wild Weekend

During the early part of my career in the escort business, when I was making rather decent money, I thought it important to show the girls my appreciation for all their hard work and loyalty. I'd take my steady A-list girls away on a girl's trip all on my dime to show them a fun time. It was my way to tell the girls "Thank you" and let them know that this was a job that would take care of them.

I had a high-roller friend of over twenty years, Bob, who helped arrange complimentary hotel rooms, dinners, and shows in Las Vegas. He was big into gambling and had connections with all of the best casinos on the strip. With his help, all I paid for was airfare, car services, and the occasional drink for our entire party. We even got comped tables at the clubs, which really got the girls into party mode. Many of the women on my roster really were all business when they were working; they didn't usually have the time to truly let loose. Now was their time to be carefree and let mother hen keep watch. The trip was usually a long weekend with about eight of my girls, who were more than ready to finally take some time for themselves.

I knew this particular weekend was about to be one for the

books right when we boarded our flight out of Newark. We were upgraded to first-class and quickly noticed the team of hockey players, some of which I already knew, eyeing us up and down. Before long, the girls were getting tipsy and subsequently flirty with our flight mates. As the jet soared higher, so did the girls' excitement to arrive in Vegas with their new sporty beaus. I'm sure the athletes were feeling good, too. What better way to prep for a tourney than to get out some sexual tension!

We were greeted on the Vegas tarmac by a stretch limo, which whisked us away to our VIP suite at the Mirage. Within the suite were several bedrooms, an enormous living room stocked with a wet bar, and a formal dining room. The clean wall of windows faced west, letting in the golden evening sunshine and, when left open, allowing for a dry, cooling breeze. The cream-colored sectional was splashed in plush teal throw pillows, giving off a somewhat beachy vibe without leaning toward the nautical. There was also a stunning steam-room shower that, later, fit seventeen drunken partiers *very* comfortably. All of us girls explored the suite and picked out bedrooms, some girls choosing to bunk with each other since they had some plans to stay close during the trip, if you know what I mean. A couple of girls, my more independent ladies of the bunch, stayed in another suite simply so everyone could spread out contentedly. After we all set our bags down, we went on to discover the outdoor pool, a small putting green, and an outdoor minibar, fully stocked with top-shelf liquor. The pool glittered from the high Las Vegas sun. It was optional to have it heated, but that was hardly necessary. We had seen all that the suite had to offer, which was quite a lot, but now it was time to get gussied up for the night ahead.

The first night was all about setting the tone for the rest of the trip, so we went out for dinner at a five-star restaurant within the Mirage before heading to Studio 54's VIP lounge. All the drinks were comped, thanks to Bob! Club music hit so heavy we could feel it in our chests as cool champagne was passed around. Glasses clinked together in celebration of a successful year for us all and for the companionship we had found in each other. The industry we were in could be so cutthroat and dangerous. There was so much room for loss and hurt if not handled professionally and seriously. Together with my girls, I had a business that thrived and women who made their own way in the world. No pimps, no coercion, and no loneliness. I looked around me and was nothing but proud and grateful for this life we had created for each other. It was the success of my life, short-lived, but entirely fulfilling.

"Well, gentleman, look who we found!" We hear a booming Slavic voice cut through the music and looked up to see a few members of the hockey team walking up to our table. Their slacks and button-downs were clearly professionally tailored to fit their athletic bodies. No way men that big were buying off the rack.

"Hi, boys," the girls said in near unison, high pitched and purring. The buzz we were all assuredly feeling by then could not mask, more likely accentuated, their hungry eyes.

The girls danced with the athletes for a bit, but we were getting bored of that club, so we gathered our boys and piled into our limo. Seventeen of us in all, we cruised on back to our Mirage villa. Things in the limo were already getting wild. One of the girls, rip-roaring drunk on bubbly, ripped her glittery top off and stuck her torso out of the sunroof, singing "God Bless America" as we sped down Las Vegas Boulevard. Passers-by hooted and hollered at the nude beauty, only fueling her belting more. The tone was set; this was sure to be a night to remember if the booze didn't black us all out.

Back at the villa, we were greeted at the back entrance by a none-too-happy butler prepared to lead us back to our suite. When the hockey players saw our place, their jaws dropped. Sure, they were being put up in a nice spot too, but nothing compared to what we had booked. It was time to make a dent in that outdoor minibar. The boys cracked open beers for them-selves and made mixed drinks for us ladies. Someone had put music on the surround sound speakers, and I strolled about, drink in hand, taking in the revelry of those around me and picking up on snatches of conversation.

"No way, you did? You gotta show us, then!" one of the girls squealed.

"It's true, he showed me pictures one time! Tell them, Marky," the accented player said as he shoved a shorter team with playfulness.

"Yeah, yeah, okay. So, I used to strip on weekends when I was still in the minors. They don't pay that great, you know!" he replied, his cheeks reddening.

After some gentle persuasion, we had Mark put on a little show for us all. He was shy at first, but soon had one of my girls, Erica, reclined on a lounge chair, grinding and stripping while his teammates cheered him on. It wasn't long before we all got to see what this shorter, cute guy was working with. Erica must've been impressed because at some point, they snuck off without the rest of the party noticing and I elected not to say anything. This was their weekend, after all! He wasn't the only one to lose his clothes, because, at this point, we were all either swimming in our skivvies or playing a rousing round of nude put-put. Remember that sauna room I mentioned earlier? It was certainly steamy in there, not just because of the warm mist pouring in.

It was like we simply couldn't sit still! A couple of girls suggested we all hit up a new late-night club, so I phoned down to the concierge to have us put on the guest list. It was a new spot, but apparently, it was all the rage since my girls had heard about it all the way in NYC. We arrived and the drinks kept coming. I was never much of a drinker, which remained true even on that trip. However, while we were at the club, I was introduced to something I'd never tried before and haven't really touched since -- ecstasy. I loved the whole world after popping that little pill, dancing, and singing with all my posse. I ended up with dozens of phone numbers from God only knows who. Some of the men we came with broke off to search for new talent. It was a good thing the girls on this trip were so capable of taking care of themselves because that night, I was nobody's babysitter. Finally, I was the one letting my hair down. It made that weekend even more special than it already was.

The following morning, everyone was hungover except me, another benefit of my brief foray into a party drug. I ordered all of us massages to be followed by a light brunch of fruits, yogurts, and bagels. The girls rose like the dead at nearly one o'clock pm, with massage therapists on stand-by. When the girls got around to eating, chatting about the previous night's revelries, I chimed in with a good idea what to do later in the day.

"They're playing at T-Mobile tonight. We should all go and cheer them on!" I said excitedly. It had been ages since I'd been to a sporting event and really, I was just dying to go, so I was hoping I could convince the girls.

"I don't even know how long hockey games usually take. Will it eat into our evening a lot?" Addison, one half of an Australian duo asked with a little bit of sass.

"Yeah, seriously," her partner, Kylie, said. "We don't wanna lose any party time, Anna."

"The game will probably be crazy fun, though," Erica chimed in, blushing. I should've known she'd be into the idea, with her little crush in the starting line-up. With her support, the other girls soon got into it, especially when I mentioned how hard the guys would be partying if they ended up winning. The suggestion turned into solid plans, so we all got started making up our faces and picking out clothes with the team's signature red, white, and blue in mind.

You can imagine the looks we got as eight bombshells, plus myself, exited a limo dressed top to bottom in designer brands.

We didn't waste time with the box seats that were offered to us. We wanted to be front and center so the boys could see us cheering for them. Every time they scored, the girls would lift their tops, jumping up and down. Needless to say, the cameras for the jumbotron were kept away from our section to avoid any indecency. I don't know much about hockey, but our team won with what seemed like a record number of goals. I thought the game was usually pretty low-scoring, but not when a group of striking women is acting as your cheerleaders for the night!

We opted for dinner at the MGM that night since we had certainly kept the Mirage staff busy the night prior. The food was to die for, luxury like I had never experienced before. It was as if every year I did this getaway, the casinos had upped the ante. We all toasted to meeting up later, around ten that night, at another club after we all caught up on some sleep. When we got to the club that night, though, we noticed the short dancer, as well as Kylie and Addison, were nowhere to be found. This put Erica right into a tizzy as she downed shots back-to-back. I heard that she and he had made plans to hook up again, but I guess those plans had gone right out the window. She got pretty shitfaced, to be frank, so me and the girls decided we should drop her back at the villa so we could continue the night without any sloppiness. It was better for everyone that way. Erica just needed to sleep off the jealousy.

What a poor decision we had made. When we opened the door to the suite, we were like deer in headlights at what was happening before our very eyes. There stood the captain of the hockey team, a big Russian brute, with Jimmy Choo's, size seven, dangling off his shoulders. The girl wore nothing else but those designer stilettos and a diamond belt as she lay on the low marble table, pounded into such elation she did not notice my surprised gasp. We all stood there awkwardly as the couple continued to go at it unfazed until someone finally snapped out of it and closed the door. We didn't have much of an option besides waiting them out in the hotel bar, and nursing cocktails until the room became more accommodating for us. One of the players with us was starting to worry because he hadn't heard from Mark. I'm sure Erica felt similarly, since we hadn't seen our two Australian girls, either. She had sobered up a bit during our wait, so I left everyone at the Mirage and made my way to the MGM to meet up with Bob. When I arrived, he was gambling away as I expected he would be. We chatted for a bit before I recalled that the Australian girls were staying at the MGM. Bob had their room number since he was the one who had it comped, so I decided to pay them a visit. They answered the door, each wearing a coy little smirk, before they giggled their way back to the king size bed. I followed them and asked what was so funny. "Are you girls feeling alright? You're awfully fidgety," I remarked.

"Yes," they giggled, then pulled the covers down to reveal our missing dancer! I suppose they'd be holed up in that room basically all night, it was such a wreck. Room service platters were strewn across table and clothing dotted the elaborate bedroom rug. Now, what happens in Vegas, stays in Vegas. I just warned them not to brag about this to Erica, best to keep it to themselves entirely, because she was quite bruised about being stood up. They understood, but still rushed me out of the room so they could enjoy the rest of their time together before the trip came to a close. I left all three and went back to my hotel, shaking my head thinking about what would happen next. Our poor drunken Erica, who was looking for the moonlighting stripper, was extremely upset at being stood up. After all, a woman with her looks and many Playboy magazines under her belt certainly does not get dumped often. I walked away as if I knew nothing, and decided in this situation, playing the role of Switzerland would be best for everyone concerned.

Eventually, we all went out again, including the Australians and their new boytoy, around two in the morning. That spacious hour is when the party really gets started on the strip. It seemed like everyone was going to be cordial, but someone let the cat out of the bag. It ended up being one of the other hockey players who had a crush on Erica. He told her about the threesome and all hell broke loose. Such high school drama, if you ask me, but this is to be expected to some degree. Still, it was my job to keep the girls out of trouble, so again I had to bring Erica back to our suite when she got belligerent off Grey Goose and green envy. With us back at our spot, the rest of the night went off without a hitch. The girls even took the hockey players to a male strip club, where our little dancer impressed even the most seasoned of the dancers there. It was a weekend to remember, even if I did have to spend the last few hours consoling a hungover model. What else is new?

# Melvin, The Carpet Man

Melvin was one of the most recognizable faces within the adult industry. He frequented strip clubs, escort services, and more. I'm not sure of anyone I was familiar with that he was not a patron of. He owned a large carpet store in the city and when closing time came around, seven p.m. sharp, he had plans with some of the hottest workingwomen I had to offer.

Whenever I think of Melvin, I smile. He was a nice man who the girls never complained about. A regular if there ever was one, he booked his appointments for 7:30 p.m. throughout the week held at one of our in-call locations. His stuttering voice was very distinct, gruff with a slight and undistinguishable accent. When he showed up in the in-call joint, all the ladies on staff that night would say hi and flirt a little. He never stayed longer than forty-five minutes, even though there was a two-hour minimum charge. It didn't bother him though, being charged for more time than he needed, and he was a true gentleman in that way.

He arrived at every booking right on time, ringing the bell and alerting us to his presence at the door. His small frame and anxious shifting made him recognizable on the security camera right away. We'd buzz him in, and he'd make his way up the stairs, glancing behind him occasionally. He had to walk rather slowly and carefully. I neglected to mention, he brought with him a huge six-foot by eight-foot carpet, rolled up with electrical tape and weighing in at nearly half his own weight. It was a burden to carry, but it was his special prop.

The floor manager walked him to the room reserved for his session and asked if he'd like anything to drink. He always declined, instead asking to see the newest hire first. All the while, he was slicking the few strands of hair he had back against his scalp and sweating from the exertion.

The floor manager left to grab whoever was new while Melvin took a boxcutter from his pocket and cut free the carpet. He rolled it out flat on the floor and did a brief walkabout on it. A lady would stop by every couple of minutes, peeking her head in and complimenting Melvin's carpet, nodding with approval. He'd shake a few hands and exchange a few hellos from his seated position in the corner of the room, assessing the girls that stopped in. The floor manager returned and asked him if anyone caught his eye. He usually picked out two ladies but was known to choose as many as four when he was having a good day. The women he picked out were thicker and tall, and he liked when they happened to be wearing pointy-toed high heels.

In the brief time he was alone again, waiting for his chosen ladies to come back, he rolled himself up into the carpet, leaving only the top of his head sticking out. I wonder how he positioned his hands after he was snug as a bug in there. I'm not sure if he could even reach his member or move much at all! Apparently, it didn't matter much to Melvin because he did this every time. The ladies walked into the room and took to stepping on the rolled-up Melvin. It started with just gentle steps and pushes, but the women soon progressed to trampling on the man up and down the length of the carpet. How bruised he must've gotten, having multiple 160-pound women jumping all over him, week after week! They could hear his muffled grunts from within the carpet, just barely able to make out his voice saying "harder". They jumped and stamped for forty-five minutes straight, never giving him a break. His grunting and the thumping around in there could be heard all down the hall and probably on the floor below. At the in-call house, this was expected ruckus and wasn't paid any mind by other patrons, though I'm sure they wondered what could possibly be going on in that room.

It was a great workout for the girls, and they really had fun with it. Melvin never wanted to see them naked during this appointment, never asked for sex at all. In fact, once he was satisfied with the carpet-play, the girls unrolled him and sat on his carpet while he began to self-gratify. He grew hard while they stroked the carpet, talking about how they loved the color and how plush and expensive it felt. As soon as he came, he wiped himself with a wet cloth and dressed in a hurry. Lots of girls received expensive gifts of jewelry and clothes from their clients, but if Melvin liked you, he gave you the carpet he brought. Not bad, when you consider such a furnishing from his store was priced at around $600. He'd also leave a cash tip on the set of drawers before he left the room and went home.

I had girls fight over those carpets quite a few times because he never specified who it was meant for when he left it. I think it was a little game he liked to play, picking out a nice accent rug like that and knowing the ladies would want to take it home. He was a clever one, that Melvin, even if his kink was a little odd.

# Fillies in the Hayloft

A long time ago, when I first started my business, I had a client who owned a massive riding establishment for Olympic-level horses with a large estate near Duchess County, New York. Charles was an older gent in his late 50's. He was recently divorced with two children who were off at university in Europe.

Every so often, he would call and ask to book two petite, preferably brunette, American college-age girls who loved the outdoors. He requested they wear floral hippy-style dresses, sandals, and no bra. He would call days in advance for a Sunday date so the girls would be fully prepared with his request. Sunday was the only day of the week his groomers left early for their day off and, thus, the only time he was able to have his entire playground to himself.

Each time, the car would pick up the two girls around 4:00 pm. The estate was a good hour and a half drive from New York City. Charles would have the girls dropped off at his beautiful multi-story white home. It had a circular driveway with a fountain in the middle, a very regal statement that reflected the interior of the estate.

Charles would greet the women in full huntsmen attire complete with a horn.

"Ladies! Welcome to my estate! Please, please come this way. We have *much* to do tonight and little time to waste!" He was undeniably in character. Though it was, at first, a bit of a silly sight, the ladies quickly adjusted and rather admired the fanfare he promoted. Charles was a true gentleman; he was odd, but a gentleman, nonetheless. He, in fact, knew how to play that horn, but there was another horn in mind that'd be getting played with that evening.

As the girls entered the home, they were offered a grand spread of English-style finger sandwiches, fresh cream and jelly, and their choice of wine or tea. Usually, to keep their wits about them, the girls would start with a few sips of wine but quickly switch to tea. He only offered the best brew, shipped directly to him from England in ornate, airtight packaging. The trio chatted about this and that, usually with Charles leading the conversation to include his expertise in riding events and, in particular, his horses' accomplishments. Many of his steeds had won both national and international circuits.

This would serve as a great segue into showing off the trophy room! Glass display cabinets were lined with dozens of trophies, crystal awards, and ribbons, each one paired with a picture of the winning horse. Charles would then pose the question: "Would you ladies like to see the stables?" Of course, the girls would oblige him, and they walked through meticulously sculpted gardens out to the state-of-the-art barn. It was a scene straight out of *Town & Country*. The stables must've been an expensive build, but it was nothing compared to the cost of its residents. Each horse was valued anywhere from a few hundred thousand to a million dollars.

With their walk through the stables underway, the girls sometimes pausing to gaze upon a horse (touching the horses was strictly prohibited) Charles would start to feel frisky. He'd take his riding crop and lift up the girls' dresses as he walked behind them. Often, to his delight, he found them to be wearing no panties. He would say "You're a racy little filly, aren't you? Are you ready for Uncle Charles?" The ladies would giggle then, skipping off toward a ladder that led to the hayloft above them. A game of hide-and-seek would ensue in the dark and dust of the loft. He removed his Jodhpur riding pants and would have a full-on erection along with a smirk from ear-to-ear. He would call to his little fillies, "Come see what a nice carrot I have for you. It's big, sweet, and juicy; the finest carrot you will ever taste. Don't be shy, my fillies."

A girl might be doing reasonably well at hiding, but a soft sneeze gave her position away and Charles would soon be upon her. The ladies could hardly see but for the light filtering in through the slatted floor. They could see Charles's shadowed silhouette, strong and short like a jockey just out of his prime. Now, Uncle Charles would perform as the stud horse and ask one girl to place a silk ribbon around the other's head and neck, holding her still as she bent over the hay bales. Charles would enter her from behind, and as a mare would do, the girl would resist slightly and cry out, but Charles would continue, as he would say, to breed her. It was a surprise to all the girls that a man of Charles's age was still able to go at it with such vigor! All the while, he would be chatting about what great breeding stock they would be and what fine offspring they would have. He actually had told women, while in this rather unique position, that he chose his ex-wife strictly based upon her genetics and her ability to sire well-bred children, and how proud he was that both his children excelled in sports and academics alike. He wouldn't be so lucky with this mare, though, since he had been shooting blanks for nearly five years by then. One could dream, I suppose.

The next game began in the pastures surrounding the estate, which was quite secluded from any neighbors. The mares in season and a chosen stud had been out to pasture to allow nature to run its course. Charles intended to do the same with his fillies. All three of them would take a walk to the bottom pasture. In the center was a small, wooded area where horses could find shade and a small running stream, which glittered endlessly under the nighttime moon.

Now for the fun part to continue. Charles was buck-naked, and the girl whom he hadn't attempted to breed in the stables was the one he must catch. He would close his eyes and count to thirty. According to his rules, she could hide anywhere within the boundaries of the pasture which was a vast twenty-five or so acres.

"Now, my dear, are you ready to help me catch our little runaway filly?" Charles asked, his hands cupping her face and pulling her close. "We wouldn't want her to get away from us for too long, would we? She's far too precious!"

"I'll bet I know where she went!" the girl clapped excitedly. Their bare feet squished in the soft grass of the field. They could see the small imprints of the lady that had run off going toward a small stand of pines by a stream.

"Careful, girl. Don't scare her off, now."

"I'll go slow," she whispered, taking Charles by the erection and leading him to his lost prize. "Hey, don't be scared. We won't hurt you." The runaway peeked out from behind a thick trunk and licked her lips.

Slowly, the other woman would try to persuade her not to run and would place the silk ribbon on her head and neck and stand holding the ribbon while Charles approached from behind. As usual, he would tell her what a fine-bred mare she was, and they would produce a champion line of offspring. When he finished off, they would stroll back home for dessert. He would reminisce about the old days and how his family molded the country with some of his finely bred horses.

The car service would come promptly at 1:00 am, as always, and safely take the women back to the city. Gentle Charles always tipped the girls an extra $1,000 each for making his night special.

You learn in my world that nothing is too strange, and most of it, you just let roll off your back with a smirk. Charles had allowed his business and passion to seep into his sexual fantasies. I truly hope it started and ended with playing pretend, but Lord only knows!

# The Uptight Weatherman

As a madam, I had many clients who were so filthy rich most of the public have never even heard of them. You'd never be able to pick them out of a lineup if your life depended on it. That made things easy for them. Others, however, had no choice but to be extremely recognizable. Those who were on TV, of course, had their whims and desires met by a woman of the night often. I mean, who has time for a family when you've got to be up at three o'clock in the morning preparing for the six o'clock news? In the early days of my business, a forward-facing, very in-the-public-eye type gent would call every few weeks looking for a redheaded woman to do a little role play with him. It would go something like this.

A stunning auburn beauty, standing around 5'10", would arrive at his one-bedroom Upper Eastside apartment a bit after dinner time which, for him, was rather early in the evening. He had to be in bed before the sun, he liked to say. He'd have his front door unlocked and the bedroom door ajar so she could let herself in while he finished showering. He was another one who was a serious germaphobe. I don't know exactly how long he spent bathing, but the girl was there for at least twenty minutes before he came out, only to breeze by her like she was invisible and strutting like a male model. He'd have to spend hours longer showering if he wanted to dim out that hideous orange tan he was known for. He closed the long, black-out curtains over his living room windows and then sat down with his date, wearing just a bathrobe. He asked if he could get her anything.

"No," she responded, remembering her scripted response. "But I was wondering if I could sit closer to you."

"Closer? Why?"

"You're just so hot. I don't think I've ever seen a man as gorgeous as you," she'd say, scooching her chair closer and leaning toward him. "Oh, wow. You smell so good."

"Please, don't get so close. I'm a married man and a good Christian!" At this point, the client would open the chest of his bathrobe to reveal a perfectly hairless, but muscular, chest. This one wasn't even married. Not yet anyway. The girl had to continue persuading him.

"Oh, please don't leave me in this state! I'm so wet for you. Even God wants you to do me. Don't you think He wants you to get what you deserve?" The redhead would be practically on her knees before him at this point. Soon, she'd have stripped down to a lacy bra and panty set, while the gent would be trying to cover her up with his robe. It only disadvantaged him, though, because now she had a full view of the proof that he liked what he was seeing. He was hard as a rock. She'd spent about thirty minutes throwing herself at him until it was time to flip the script. Now, she had to beg for his forgiveness, that she was a terribly naughty girl for trying to seduce him.

"I'm such a sinner. How will God forgive me for being such a whore!" She'd sit on the edge of the bed, sniffling out some fake little sobs.

"No, no," he reassured her. "You're no worse than anyone. God made Adam and Eve. He made the forbidden fruit. We shouldn't deprive ourselves of the pleasure that God makes available to us," he'd say, all the while stroking himself and undressing the girl further. "Maybe I was being hasty earlier. Maybe making love is not so sinful."

"I've never made love before," she teased.

"No?"

"No. I've only ever been fucked. Fucked hard in my tight little pussy like a bad, bad girl." She looked up at him with doe eyes, pushing out her bottom lip just a smidge.

"Hmm. I think that's all bad girls like you deserve," he said, turning from her and pulling open a drawer from the side table. Inside, he pulled out a little pill bottle and dumped one into the palm of his hand. A rhombus in robin's egg blue.

Then he'd have her in every way possible. Two hours in and the girl would basically have to sprint out the door, grabbing her fee on the way out. She'd take the next day or two off to recover from all that friction, since the jerk never bothered to invest in some lube. I'll tell you, God created sex, but the Devil made Viagra. That stuff is every working girl's nightmare. And after all that time, with every girl he exhausted, he never left a dime more than the fee. The girls he booked deserved millions after the coldhearted pounding he gave them. It always seemed to be like that; the easy ones are generous, and the cheap ones always want more than they should take. One girl even told me that after running through the script, while they were getting it on, he couldn't stop staring into the mirror positioned next to the bed. I guess he really liked what he saw, in himself that is!

A few weeks after he had an appointment, I got a call while sitting in my living room. It was the redhead he booked, telling me to put on the news.

"That's him! That's the cheap Christian who's always hopped up on Viagra!" she yelled into the phone.

Sure enough, that was him, telling me that it was going to rain all weekend. Just another reason to think this orange bozo was destined to be the bearer of only bad news.

# Three Isn't Always a Crowd

Nearly eleven years ago, I had a client named Steve who was always a perfect gentleman. He booked with us regularly throughout the year, usually preferring someone tall, under thirty years old, who possessed all the typical runway model attributes. Steve lived on two full floors of an Upper Eastside apartment on Park Avenue. It was well within his price range as he was the chairman and CEO of a private equity and financial advisory firm. One year, I can't quite remember when, he was listed among Time Magazine's top 100 Most Influential People. One can imagine how much the girls he booked through us were making, even if he only booked them one time.

Steve was a detail-oriented man, a very type-A personality as is common for financiers. He'd call me a day or so in advance, making a point to do so when his wife was not around, to book his girl and get a date scheduled. If he booked someone a bit newer, there was a bit of intimidation or hesitancy she felt once she found out who he was. He ran in powerful political circles from New York City to the White House. To me and my seasoned veterans, he was just Steve, a man with some money and a terribly nasty habit of letting his toenails grow out. Seriously, he sounded like a dog on tile walking around barefoot. This quirk was usually the only complaint girls had about him.

There was one time that things went about differently with Steve. He rang me up and asked if he could make a special request. I was to act as though we had never spoken before the next time he called me, to pretend that he had gotten my number from a friend of his. I told him I understood, and that would be fine.

I got his call a few days later. Steve had a woman on the line with him, so I played the part as we had discussed. I said, "May I ask how you got this number?" When Steven responded by saying a friend gave it to him, I informed him that he would have to have his friend call on his behalf so I could confirm his trustworthiness. We ended the call then, but Steve followed up the next day, the woman still on the line with him, and I said "Thank you for your patience, Steve. As I'm sure you can understand, I only work through reliable referrals." Thus, the ruse was complete, and Steven could get on with making his real request.

Steven introduced me to the woman with him as his wife. Yes, that made sense. Together, they explained their plan to take their yacht to the south of France, then to Italy, and needed a companion to bring with them. They wanted it to be a most memorable experience so they would need this companion for the duration of their trip, about a week.

"We'll fly her out, first-class. Her days would be her own, of course. All the shopping and sightseeing is free to her, as well as full access to the amenities on board," Steve explained. It sounded like a once-in-a-lifetime vacation to me. I'd be lying if I said I wasn't a little jealous! I knew I would have quite the job picking the right girl while keeping things hush-hush, so my entire roster didn't go up in arms about not being chosen.

I started calling around, putting together a list of ladies for Steve and his wife to choose from. I set up a casting so the couple could meet their potential matches personally and decide who they connected with best. All in all, they met about fifteen girls before settling on Pam, a tall brunette with really arresting hazel eyes. She was so excited to be chosen and got packing right away. I gave her the usual spiel, making her promise she would call daily. I got the name of the yacht and its planned route from Steve.

Pam arrived as planned and was taken below deck to a luxury cabin. On board, other than the couple and Pam, were crewmen, chefs, and two masseuses. So, the trip was private, but not that private. It must've been a total staff of around twenty people just attending to three individuals. I can't imagine what they all thought of their boss at the conclusion of the trip, but I bet it wasn't exactly fond. As fate would have it, Pam and Steve's wife, Martha, both wore blue dresses and white sandals that first night. The atmosphere grew rather chilly for the south of France in mid-July.

Dinner was served and conversation was stunted throughout. Steve let Pam know that he and the wife were going to go ashore to meet up with some socialites also in the area. There was an active nightlife and Pam was not invited but was free to spend the evening on board however she pleased.

"I'm happy to come with you if you'd like!" Pam expressed.

"No. Not tonight," Martha responded firmly. They departed and a dejected Pam spent the evening reading alone.

The following morning, the trio sat down for breakfast together, with Martha seeming to be in much better spirits. At one point, Pam even caught Martha looking at her with hungry eyes. Steve reached for his wife's hand and, turning to Pam, said "We may ring your cabin, in an hour or two, for you to join us in our suite." Pam nodded and left the table to get ready for their rendezvous. Several hours went by, but finally, Pam was summoned to the suite. The door was cracked open a bit so Pam could just see on the corner of the bed a lovely, pedicured foot. Pam pushed the door open further, discovering Steve in just a towel and Martha laid out on the king-sized bed, nude and spread eagle. Pam was slightly embarrassed, not because of her expected participation in a threesome (she was wondering when they would finally approach her and was delighted when they did), but because it seemed they had accidentally left the shade on the window open for all the crew to see into the suite. Her flushed cheeks must've tipped Steve off, but he just chuckled and said "We like to keep things open. Very open," and led Pam to the space between his wife's legs. Pam knew all too well that the richer they were, the odder, and got started on doing what she came there to do. Martha.

The women moaned together, kissing and touching while Steve watched with fervor. Soon, he slipped a condom on, got behind Pam, and joined them in their indulgence. It was a scene right out of Nubile Films, the Mediterranean Sea lapping lightly at the side of the boat as crewmen passed the suite window with consciously averted eyes. It was all well and good until Steve opened his big mouth.

"You have such a beautiful ass, and you're so tight," he exhaled into Pam's ear. I suppose he didn't say it quietly enough because, like a bolt of lightning, Martha sat up, grabbed the lamp next to the bed, and flung it at Steve's head. Pam just barely dodged the fixture and ran out of the room with breathless abandon, donning nothing but an anklet!

The couple must've fought for the better part of an hour, all the while pam listening just down the hall to all the yelling. A deckhand came by the check on Pam, inquiring if she needed anything, to which she replied with a curt "No, thank you". It was getting truly annoying for Pam to just sit in her room alone, but she figured it had been quiet long enough for her to try venturing out to the top deck to try and catch a late afternoon tan. Slipping into a barely-there bikini, Pam was all but settled into the deck chair when the same man that had come by her room earlier informed her that she could not be on the top deck while

Martha was using it. Pam asked if she could take out one of the jet skis then, but was met with an apologetic no, not unless Martha and Steve are ashore. Pam huffed but returned to her room without making a scene. I cannot say I would've blamed her if she had thrown a bit of a fit at this point, but I admire and appreciate her professionalism to this day.

Dinner was uncomfortable to say the least, even more silent than the first night. Even so, Steve asked Pam to join them in the suite again after the evening turndown service. Pam agreed, retiring to her room until called upon, left to ponder what catastrophe might await her this time. The only way out, in Pam's mind, was to jump ship and swim for shore if anything went too awry. Of course, if she had called, I would've moved hell to get her back home.

She had a great plan, though. Once Steve called her, she went to Martha right away, caressing her neck and saying how much she'd been thinking about her. "I prefer women, anyway," she whispered into Martha's ear. This method certainly alleviated much of the tension, while Steve was much more of a spectator than a participant this time around. The session went smoothly, though Pam was still dismissed abrasively once Martha had finished with her. No cuddles or pillow talk required for this couple. Much to Pam's delight, the couple went ashore early the following morning. She could finally top off her tan and take a spin on those jet skis, as she had been promised! The crew all gave her such sorrowful looks, though, and Pam decided it was finally time to call me and spill the beans on how horribly the trip was really going.

"I was wondering when I'd hear from you, sweetheart! How is everything going?"

"Uhm, I should've called you sooner. It's really bad, Anna," Pam said, practically whispering.

"What! Why? I thought it sounded like a dream!"

"Me too! And I was really looking forward to this job, but

it's been completely insane basically the whole time I've been here! They've been in fight after fight, and Martha definitely has a problem with me being here, or at least with me being with Steve. She threw a lamp at him while we were having sex!"

"Oh my God, were you hurt? When was this?"

"No, no, I'm fine. I don't know, all the days have melded together because I've been forced to stay in my cabin unless they *request my presence*. I think I want to come home, but I don't know how I would even do it. I'm stuck here!" she said and began to cry.

I was appalled! All this time, Pam had been walking on eggshells a thousand miles from home and I had it in my mind that she was having the time of her life. I could hear in her voice that she was at her wits' end. I quickly made arrangements to get my girl back to the States. Steve tried to make excuses and apologies when I called to let him know of Pam's departure, but it simply didn't matter. She was on a flight that same day. Steve paid the full fee plus a sizable tip as an apology to Pam, and I suppose it worked. He and Pam went on many more dates and Steve continued to book with me or my partner, Vera, out in London. Oddly enough, his wife booked with me on one occasion with a centerfold model that was totally her type. Apparently, they weren't the threesome type, but Steven really wanted them to be. He had to accept the fact that Martha could handle knowing what he was up to, but she couldn't bear to see it. She loved him too much and didn't want to share their intimacy. Those outside relationships were for physicality only, forbidden from mixing with their commitment to one another. Martha and Steve went on to celebrate many anniversaries, content with their unlikely arrangement.

# A Nobleman's Secret

One might recall the Eliot Spitzer scandal, in which the New York City Governor was found to be patronizing an elite escort service known as Emperors Club VIP. Spitzer became known as "Client 9", inevitably leading to the public's curiosity as to who might be Client 6, 13, et cetera.

It was rumored a certain English nobleman might be one such client. He denied the accusation adamantly, that such an accusation was an insult to himself, his family, and most certainly his ego. Unfortunately, his words totally conflicted with his brazen actions. Men like him believe rules do not apply to them. To my astonishment, when the frenzied media outed his name, he succeeded in having newspapers throughout the world retract their stories that he had been a client at all, let alone that he had been a client caught on tape. This news would have normally been absolutely front-page headlines! He used his status and power to make the whole thing disappear, left to be murmured about as if it were only an outlandish conspiracy theory.

You would think, after such a serious accusation, the Nobleman would try to lie low for a little bit while things simmered down. The Nobleman was not the kind of man who could sit still, however, and he immediately holed up in Hungary with two Hungarian models. He partied up a storm the entire time the news was breaking, only pausing to seemingly contact his PR staff so they could get to work keeping tabloids hushed. Vera, in our London office, was never alerted of his scandal by the Nobleman himself nor anyone else. We had no idea the rumored client of Emperors Club VIP and the man we'd had as a regular client for many years at that point were one and the same. So many of our clients had status like the Nobleman did; we were in the habit of looking past that, only knowing these men for their preferences and behavior towards our girls. If they never caused trouble with us, it wasn't our business to dig around in their personal affiliations. Sure, we usually ended up knowing who they were pretty well after many years of servicing them. In this case, we simply didn't know about the scandal he was involved in until the rumors finally reached us many months later.

This client's audacious acts had been established long before the scandal broke. When he booked through the London office, he often had girls brought directly to his personal residence, which was a manor that his family nearly always occupied. He was very into tall women, five foot ten or more, and we introduced him to a particular model he took a special liking to. He would have her over to his home, allowing her to use a private entrance that his family almost never utilized. He had his sentry notified so they could let her in discreetly as soon as she arrived. It was all so risky, so illicit, that I cannot believe the man had the gall to do something like this. As if he was not begging enough to get caught, he even took her out in public, affectionately leading her around the city and buying her expensive gifts. It truly seemed like the risk of getting caught was the biggest turn-on to him. Well, I imagine he might've changed his tune before it all caught up with him. It's too bad, really. He was a constant client for us, spending thousands upon thousands of pounds in London with Vera's office.

Like I said, we had no idea he was embroiled in such public indignity. When I came across his original application for our website, I was shocked by his true identity and the caliber of who, exactly, we were dealing with. Hopefully, my revealing all this doesn't get me barred from England forever. I wish I could go on about it; my dedication to confidentiality paired with my cautious approach to clientele like this prevents me from revealing any more than the fact that yes, we booked for the infamous Nobleman.

# Date with a Hitman

One day, a long-time regular, Daniel, called me to make a new request. He mentioned that his best friend was going to be in town, so he was looking to book two fun, nice girls for a two-day getaway to Vegas. I asked if his friend had a type or if it was more of a lowkey outing that didn't require anyone special. He responded: "Well, he's a hitman. Avi runs an Israeli government program that trains assassins for missions in enemy territory. I think he'd like someone who can handle a man of his intensity." Great, I thought. No pressure at all. Let it be known that hitmen were not my usual clientele.

I figured he might prefer a strong-willed woman, someone with a little fire. I matched him with Casey who, years later, I saw on a Dr. Drew rehab program. Nevertheless, when she was working for me, she was an honest and good-hearted woman. For my regular gent, I booked his usual favorite, Madeline.

Before the girls jetted off to sin city, I gave them both a bit of a warning. "This is a VIP trip, ladies," I said. "So, no shenanigans. We must make a good impression with this new gent." Madeline had little concern for the trip, what with her having spent plenty of time with Daniel. Casey, on the other hand, was a bit nervous. I didn't reveal that he was a hitman, per se, because I didn't want to scare the poor things. I just told them that he worked for the Israeli government as a military official. I figured that should be information enough for the girls to understand who they were out with.

The girls arrived at Newark for their first-class flight to Las Vegas. Casey, our fierier of the pair, gets her luggage stowed away, finds her seat, and buckles up. Madeline was rather petite and had a difficult time fitting her luggage in its designated compartment.

"'Scuse me, could you help me with this?" Madeline said, gesturing from her suitcase to the overhead space.

"I'm a little busy right now, ma'am," the steward said as he looked up and down the aisle, chewing gum rather noisily.

"I can't lift it, though. A man's help would be greatly appreciated."

"Oh, honey, you got the wrong one. Now if you can't get it up there yourself, we'll have to check it and add the charge."

"It'll fit, I mean seriously, I just need some assistance. Isn't that your job?" Madeline questioned him, beginning to feel a bit helpless and allowing a whine to seep into her tone.

"Lady, I don't know what crawled into your panties today, but I'm really not in the mood for it! Take your bag and your bad attitude and get back to the terminal."

"What! You're gonna check the bag even though it'll fit right here?" The space stood gaping, seemingly wider than when Madeline originally attempted to put her bag away. Mockingly empty it remained.

"I'm not checking your bag; I'm removing you from this flight. You're clearly gonna be a troublemaker." The steward cocked his head and turned on his heel in order to alert the captain that they may need security.

"Fine, fine! I'll go..." Madeline said, looking desperately from seat to seat in search of Casey. She had headphones on and couldn't hear Maddy calling her name. Finally, she got her attention and told her what was happening, but Casey had little to say in response and Maddy was led by the elbow off the plane by the smug looking steward. All this, twenty minutes before they were meant to take off.

I was blindsided by Casey's call, where she told me that Madeline had been kicked off the flight, but she was still seated and ready to take off.

"What? No!" I yelled into the phone. "You two should stay together!"

"Oops. Well, it's too late now. We just pulled away from the gate and the steward is telling me to put my phone away. Sorry, Anna, I gotta go," Casey said and hung up. I hadn't even had time to think about what to do next before my phone was ringing again, now with Maddy's name illuminating my screen.

"Anna, I…I got booted off the flight!" Maddy hyperventilated between words, and I could hardly say anything to get her to calm down. Eventually, I got her quieted enough to listen to the plan. I told her she needed to go talk to a supervisor for the airline and explain the situation. Maddy got herself together, went and talked to someone, and got them to put her on the next possible flight free of charge. She'd be about two hours behind Casey, but that should still give her enough time to get ready and make it to their date.

Casey actually had a place in Henderson, about twenty minutes from the Strip. She went straight from the airport to her residence to get ready and let Maddy know she was welcome to do the same once she landed. Maddy really pulled off a miracle, and both our ladies arrived at dinner on time for what I heard was an elegant and enjoyable meal. Afterward, Daniel wanted to do some gambling, but Avi wasn't in the mood. Instead, he asked if the ladies would like to show him around the city, to which they happily obliged. The remainder of that first night went swimmingly, with Daniel happy to have some time at the poker tables and the trio hitting up various clubs and getting to know each other.

It was the second night that things went a little haywire. Casey, our bad Barbie, decided it would be appropriate to have some forbidden party goods delivered to the suite they were all staying in. That's always a big no-no in my books, but what I don't know can't hurt me, in Casey's mind. I was operating under the assumption that everything was still going well and that the trip would wrap up nicely in the morning. I went to bed around eleven p.m. that night, happy that I could trust two experienced girls with high-profile clients.

Sometime later, I woke up to my phone ringing. I bolted upright when I answered and heard Maddy once again sobbing on the phone.

"Casey attacked me! That fucking bitch is high as shit and got all offended over nothing."

"Maddy, calm down. What did you say to her?" I asked.

"We were all partying and fucking and whatever, when Avi asked me what I thought of Casey's pussy. I said it was okay, what else am I supposed to think, but she freaked out and came at me, pulling my hair like a psycho!"

I was at a loss for words. Maddy went on explaining how she had herself locked away in the bathroom, that she only got away after Avi and Daniel had yanked Casey off her.

The phone was beeping, alerting me to a call waiting, and I was half expecting to hear Avi or my regular on the other end. Instead, it was Casey. She said, "That rude, ungrateful, fucking bitch. I want to throw her out of the penthouse window. She insulted my pussy. Can you imagine?" I really didn't know what to say at this point. I tried to calm her down and asked her to go back to her place in Henderson since we didn't want hotel security coming up and arresting both of them. I asked Maddy to stay there until Casey left, so she didn't get the chance to clobber her to death in the elevator on the way out of the hotel. The two split up, and about an hour later, Casey called and said, "Tell that bitch she has thirty minutes to pick up her shit, or it will be curb-side." So, we had to send a car service to Henderson to get Maddy's luggage to safety. Maddy stayed in Vegas until Sunday and left on her pre-booked flight.

I was left waiting for the fallout from Daniel and Avi being upset that their special weekend was ruined by a temper tantrum. A few days went by without hearing anything, and I assumed Daniel and Avi were too angry to even speak to me about what happened. I didn't want to call them first because I didn't want to overstep boundaries, nor was I looking forward to the chewing out I was bound to get. It was a bit cowardly, I know, but remember Avi's profession. Excuse me for being a little hesitant to speak to him about the issue. Then, out of the blue, Daniel called and said "Hey, I just wanted to thank you. Avi had a great time and can't wait to get back to the states to do it again! He really liked Casey. Hold onto her for him!" I laughed, nervously accepting the gratitude. I guess I picked the right girl, after all! However, I kept it in mind that she and Maddy could not be booked together again. I'd have to find Daniel someone new when his hitman friend came around looking for some fun. If you ask me, the whole thing could've been avoided if Casey hadn't indulged in whatever got her so fired up, but at least it all worked out!

# Height of Professional Standards

I had this gent who could be extremely difficult in his own unique way, yet there was a pleasant side that I liked. Call it a love/hate relationship.

His story was quite historical in its own right. He was a seasoned fighter pilot who flew one of the planes in "Operation Opera" in 1981. His squad blew up Iraq's nuclear reactor that Saddam acquired from the French. After he had served in the Israeli military, he moved to America and hit it big during the dot-com bubble. He had a great passion for collecting planes.

I would allow him to run his tab up a bit and then collect directly from him. I only did this for a select few clients. On one occasion, he had seen four or five ladies for multiple hours at a time, and the bill was higher than my comfort level allowed for, but I couldn't attend to him for a few days following the booking because I was going to be spending some much-needed time with my family. However, I noticed as the bill ran higher, he became more and more difficult.

He would often call weekly to see what I was doing more often than to see about the ladies. As wealthy as he was, I believe in some way, he was bored and lonely, seeking something to fill a void. If he would call and I was not on the phones, he would demand I call him back immediately. This went on for some time. Even when I told him I would be overseas or out of reach for three days, ensuring he was always in the loop about my availability, sure as the sun rises, he would call on the days I was unreachable just to bust my aunt's chops. I'm not entirely sure why, but he really disliked my bookers. I think he'd just gotten so used to working with me that he was uncomfortable dealing with anyone else. I trusted my bookers very much, but I really didn't allow anyone to book my big clients; it was my responsibility. Yet, as I've mentioned, I did have to take time off every now and again when it was completely necessary. Perhaps the infrequency of those times made my billionaires spoiled. I never was good at telling them "no."

As I said, I had plans with family, and it was a significant event. I had no time to socialize with the gents on the phone during the preparation for this event. He called my office and reached my aunt but asked for me. She told him today that of all days I certainly wouldn't be available. He became angry, cursing and hanging up on her before she could even ask how she could be of service. He never gave her the chance. If my voice wasn't the first thing he heard, he became irate.

He called the next day only to be told yet again I was not reachable, but he knew this already. He ripped into my aunt, reducing her to tears. He told her he would never work with me again since I would not take his calls, and she should let me know that. She did so, and I guess he got what he wanted because I called him right away to find out who in the world he thought he was.

I called him up, and he started off coyly asking, "Why didn't you call me back? I was trying to reach you."

"Let me remind you, I needed time off for a family affair. I was in no position to speak with anyone from work since it would have been inappropriate."

"If you don't want my business, then I'll take it elsewhere," he said.

"Suit yourself. Maybe you need someone who will eat and breathe waiting on you hand and foot, but I have four children and a life."

"Your aunt is rude, and I don't like talking to her."

"Maybe you shouldn't call her at all since you have no right bullying her and making her cry. Why don't you send me the balance of your tab, and that will conclude this relationship? Good luck finding someone who will be more attentive than me. Obviously, we couldn't fill your needs or your expectations."

"Why should I give you a check if you're the one breaking things off with me?"

"Because you were happy and had an amazing time with all those ladies so you should pay. I also trusted you with a running tab, which I rarely do. So please, do not call me again until you've decided to pay and perhaps have learned how to be a gentleman." Then, I hung up.

The very next day I saw on the caller ID that he was calling. I cringed and answered. He said, "I have your check, and I just got a new plane. I will fly to Newburgh and drop it off for you in an hour. Can you meet me?"

"Yes, thank you," I replied.

"I have one final request, before our professional relationship comes to a close. I want to take you for a spin in my new plane."

I hated flying, and he knew this. Of course, I wanted my check and wasn't happy about the possibility of losing him as a regular. The thought of flying in a plane with him made me queasy, but maybe if I obliged him, he'd change his behavior and I could keep him as a customer. I reluctantly agreed to his terms and headed up to Newburgh to the private hangar area.

When I arrived, I was expecting to see a brand-new jet with monogrammed leather seats, a fully stocked kitchenette, and staff. I looked around for something that would fit such a description but saw nothing remotely close. He tapped me on the shoulder and said, "Anna, this way." He had on a leather jacket with goggles pushed up into his hairline. We walked for a bit, and he took me to a bright yellow snoopy-like plane. It basically had two holes with seats in them.

I looked at him and said, "No way, absolutely no way. Are you joking me? There's no roof!" I knew he was getting off from my fear by the smirk on his face, but by this time I felt that a deal was a deal. I did say I would go up for a spin.

He opened a little cargo area on the side and offered me a leather jacket, goggles, and earphones with a mic. I attempted to climb in the back, but he said, "No, I sit in the back since I am piloting. You sit in the front." Holy shit! I was sitting in the front seat being strapped in and realized I was in a replica of a World War I plane. I was thinking this might be the last time I take a flight for the rest of my life because I might not live to step foot on earth again.

We took off, and you could feel how light the front was. As the plane lifted slowly off the tarmac and into the air, you could hear the engine straining as the space between me and the solid ground grew higher. I was petrified, and we had just begun. We got up to a steady altitude where I saw familiar roads and farms, even some people in a hot air balloon. I had to admit, that was pretty cool. I was beginning to relax when he chuckled and said, "Let's see what this baby can really do." I thought we were already seeing what it could do! He lifted the nose upwards, getting higher before he flipped the plane up and then down, and all I see is my life flashing before me as I scream at the top of my lungs. He shut my mic off and took me on a topsy-turvy terror ride. We did spins and nosedives. I was held hostage in my very own airshow. He laughed and continued to toss us left and right for a good fifteen minutes until we landed as smooth as could be. I had torn the belt off before the plane fully stopped and turned around to curse him out.

"Whoa, whoa, slow down, Anna. Aren't you going to compliment my piloting skills?" he laughed. As I stalked up to him, fuming, he pulled a thick envelope from the inside of his jacket and handed it to me. "No hard feelings, I hope. I call you soon," he said. He left me on the tarmac, my heart still thudding in my ears. So, he paid his debt and got a laugh out of it in the process.

The next time he called, he was much more polite and our relationship sort of fell into its previous pattern.

Sadly, I learned many years later that he lost a major part of his vision and could no longer fly due to the effect the G-force had on the retina from flying fighter planes. He scared the shit out of me that time he took me for a ride, but he was a good man, overall. He didn't really deserve that, and I wish him well.

# Revenge on the Phone Freak

My aunt did help me a lot during the times when I was busy, and it was much appreciated. But I was beginning to understand that I needed to expand my portfolio, in a sense. I set out to learn the land development trade and, in doing so, needed to hire someone to help with some administrative tasks. I hired a young man, trustworthy with an education, to man the phones and assist with bookings. Tyler was trained on how to screen new callers and was fully aware of how important it was we only send girls out with men who were safe and traceable.

One evening, during his shift, a gent called saying he would be in the city on a business trip. He said his name was Mr. McKinney, calling from South Carolina, and he'd be staying at the Hilton, which was also the place hosting the company conference. Tyler put him through the screening process after confirming with the hotel that there was, in fact, a conference that weekend for a South Carolina-based company. The screening took about forty-five minutes and Mr. McKinney passed with flying colors. He was booked with a lovely young woman, Kaitlyn, who had always been a delight and easy to work with. I often sent her out with new clients because of her easy-to-please demeanor and multiple years' experience in the business.

Kaitlyn was dropped off and strode into the hotel lobby, heading straight for the phone available to guests. She called up to Mr. McKinney's room to let him know she had arrived and to find out if he'd be meeting her in the hotel bar.

"If it's okay with you," he started, "could you come up to the room for cocktails? Many of my coworkers are staying here and might see us in the bar."

"Yeah, I think that'd be fine. Let me just make a quick call,"

"Sure, sure. Hope you don't keep me waiting too long, sweetheart," he said before the phone line went dead in Kaitlyn's ear. The sound of his voice had sent a chill through her body, but she chalked it up to nerves. It had never happened to her before, though. She dialed my number.

"Hey, Anna?"

"You get to the hotel okay?"

"Yeah, totally fine. Mr. McKinney asked if I'd come up to his room instead of meeting at the bar like we planned. He said he didn't want his coworkers to see us together. Would that be okay?"

"Makes sense. It's fine with me as long as you feel comfortable with it."

"I'm fine with it," she said after a couple moments.

"You're sure?"

She sighed. "Mm-hmm. Yes."

"Okay. Well, have a nice time!"

"Yup. Thanks, Anna," and she hung up.

I felt like she was holding something back, but how was I to know? The phone made my work possible, helped everything run smoothly, but it certainly couldn't be considered the most ideal form of communication. I couldn't see Kaitlyn; I couldn't see the way her eyebrows had scrunched together quizzically. And even if we had been talking face to face, I wouldn't have been able to see the flush at the base of her throat or the way her pulse had quickened ever so slightly. The signs are not always so clear. The client's request seemed reasonable to us both, Mr. McKinney feeling a bit uncomfortable by the prospect of being seen with a lady of the night, or any lady for that matter. He wasn't married, but many clients like to keep things secret, anyway. Nothing obviously strange could have been detected.

Kaitlyn made her way to his room on the fourth floor. She knocked and heard Mr. McKinney shout from inside, "Just a moment! I'm just getting out of the shower!" A few ticks of the second hand later, Mr. McKinney opened the door wearing just a white towel wrapped around his waist, his halfway aroused member peeking through the split in the fabric. Kaitlyn, trying to be as polite and understanding as possible, attempted to ignore his indecency as she stepped into the room. He offered her a drink which she accepted with averted eyes.

If you assumed that this was normal or expected behavior of a new client, you'd be sorely mistaken. In my service, new clients were expected to act politely as the girl got to know them, making sure things were comfortable and safe before services were rendered. There was a step-by-step process. We check the physical ID such as credit cards, driver's license, business cards, passport, and electronic tickets. Then, the exchange of funds is placed on the table. Mr. McKinney seemed intent on bypassing this part of the process, so Kaitlyn told him she needed to get in touch with the office briefly before they could proceed. He was reluctant to allow the call, attempting to distract her with conversation. As he spoke, Kaitlyn noticed his hand drifting down to his inner thigh, then to his genitals. He cupped and fondled himself, never breaking eye contact with her. Something was definitely off about this client.

He suddenly stood and removed his towel entirely. He tried to be seductive, but it all came off so clumsily and awkward.

"Come on, baby, touch me. We can have a good time together if you'd just loosen up," he said gruffly.

"I really should call my office. I forgot to tell them something earlier," Kaitlyn whispered, trying to sound sure of herself,

"Breaking the rules is what this is all about, isn't it? A little slut like you ought to know that." Mr. McKinney got right up behind where Kaitlyn was sitting then, and she felt his hard penis poke into her shoulder.

"Just gimme a minute," she said as she jumped, then stood and ran into the bathroom. "C'mon, C'mon," she said to herself as the phone rang in her ear.

"Hello?"

"Tyler? It's Kaitlyn."

"Oh, hey. How's your appointment going?" Tyler asked. He was on the phones while I took my kids to soccer that evening.

"I don't think things are going well. This guy is turning out to be kind of a creep."

"Put him on with me, I'll handle it."

"Mr. McKinney?" Kaitlyn called as she cracked the bathroom door open, "my office needs to talk with you!"

"Why? I'm not doing anything wrong."

"It'll just be a second."

"No way. Now why don't you come out of there and give me what I paid for." He started to approach the bathroom, so Kaitlyn slammed the door in his face.

"He won't talk to you. He's really making me worried now."

"Just get out of there. Anna will comp you for your time," Tyler assured her.

"I don't even care at this point. I'll let her know when I'm back home," and they stayed on the phone as Kaitlyn made her way out.

When she opened the bathroom door, McKinney was still standing there, erect and groaning at her. She was disgusted with him and said nothing as she rushed into the hallway, but he started to chase her, masturbating furiously. She was nearly running at that point and suddenly felt something warm and wet hit the back of her calves. She didn't know whether McKinney had cum in his hands and splattered it toward her or if it was just a horrifically lucky shot, but she let out a disgusted "ugh!" and ran into the elevator. McKinney, thank God, didn't try to follow her in.

Unfortunately, this happens on occasion. We get a phone freak whose whole plan is to waste the girl's time. It's frustrating because she gets dressed, made up, takes a cab, and when she arrives, it's just a phone freak. We kept McKinney and men like him in a blacklist that I had accumulated over the years and added his cell number, the company information, and hotel information with a detailed account of his despicable behavior.

Several months went by and the incident was no longer on the forefront of my mind. I'd spoken to Kaitlyn about it, meeting at a little café in the city to talk things over and comfort her. She said it wasn't the worst thing she'd been through, but she'd come to expect more of my clients and needed to be promised this wouldn't happen again. I told her we always do the very best we can with our screening process, but if she liked, we could reserve her for well-known clients only. No more new guys. She was happy about the arrangement and didn't go on any dates with newbies for several months after. Eventually, though, she stopped wanting to miss out on those very lucrative opportunities. It all ended well, at least.

We happened upon a busy week sometime later, the phones ringing off the hook daily. It must've been around a summer holiday of sorts. Nevertheless, I'll admit the hectic nature of that time made me less alert than I normally was. I picked up the phone to a man with a very pleasant voice calling about an ad we had posted. He said he was going to be staying at the Hilton for a company meeting and that his name was Mr. McKinley. I ran his information through our database and nothing of note came up. I went through with the rest of the screening and booked him with a Brazilian woman, Elena, who lived only a few blocks away from the hotel.

The only stipulation McKinley had was a wish that Elena would meet him directly in his room rather than in the hotel bar because he didn't want his boss seeing them together. Even then, I had been doing business in the escort industry for years. I prided myself on my ability to sniff out trouble, even just the faintest whiff. I was completely unaware of the mistake I was making.

Elena arrived, knocked on the door, and no one answered. I called the room for her, and Mr. McKinley said "My apologies, I was in the shower. I'm answering the door now." When he opened the door, he was standing there with just a towel slung around his neck, completely nude and visibly aroused. Elena, unlike Kaitlyn, was not to be trifled with. Upon seeing Mr. McKinley, she said, "Cover yourself. This is no way for a gentleman to act." He didn't listen and tried to get Elena to touch him, grabbing her hand when she refused. Elena was the kind of working girl that wouldn't even smile until she was paid upfront, and Mr. McKinley had made a grave misstep trying to take advantage of her.

"You're a disgusting pig," Elena said as she stormed out the door and down the hall.

"Come on, sweetie. Why don't you come back and help me feel good," Mr. McKinley hollered, chasing her down the hall until she was in the elevator. Elena called me from there and told me what happened; I was pissed. Things finally clicked and I realized just a slight change of last name helped McKinney to slip through the cracks, allowing this indecency to happen again. Thank God my girls had not been seriously hurt, but even this waste of time was enough to enrage me. After I got off the phone with Elena, I made a call to the Hilton.

I got security on the phone and explained: "I run an escort

service. Mr. McKinley in room 414 had a dinner date arranged through my company, but when the woman arrived, he answered the door completely nude with an erection, then proceeded to chase her down the hallway when she tried to escape his disgusting advances. I'm sure you don't want a sexual predator roaming your halls exposing himself to other guests. I suggest you review your security footage since I've heard from other agencies he has done this sort of thing at your hotel multiple times now. I want to go on record that you've now been alerted of this dangerous man because soon enough, he's going to escalate his behavior. You'd better do something about this before he rapes or kills someone. Now please, give me your name in case I have to bring this to the police."

I recorded the security officer's name, and he told me they would call me right back. About forty minutes later, I got a call from the Hilton's head of security, and they told me they reviewed the tape from the hallway monitor, and it confirmed everything I had told them. They threw Mr. McKinney out of the hotel, and he was banned from Hilton Hotels worldwide.

Then next morning I sent a fax to McKinney's boss outlining the events. I included the security officer's name and number. I detailed that perhaps Mr. McKinney needs more work since he's been using his spare time to prey on innocent women during business trips *he's* funded. I never heard from him again...

# Superbowl Sam

I used to love the Superbowl! I'm not the biggest football fan, but it was an amazing time of year back when I was in business. I could make in one weekend what someone else was making for the entire year. Every year, I'd fly out my A-list girls to Las Vegas for Superbowl events. They'd meet prospective clients that tagged along with the regulars, and I'd be booked solid for weeks afterwards. It was an all-around hyped-up time and when that happens, people love to have hot women hanging around, feeding off the masculine energy.

I had a regular client who hosted a great Superbowl party in Vegas. His name was Sam, and while he booked normal dates throughout the year, there were two times of the year he went all out: the Superbowl and his Summer kick-off yacht party.

For the Superbowl, he'd call me a bit before the holidays rolled around to start planning. Sam was an easy-going guy who just liked to have a good time; he booked four ladies for some classic football fun. I'd get all their travel set up and, once the teams were decided, I'd order two jerseys from each team, helmets, knee socks and, of course, sexy color-coordinated thongs. These ladies were in for the time of their lives.

The highly anticipated weekend finally arrived and Sam, along with a few friends, occupied a high-roller villa at the Mirage. The three-bedroom suite had a gorgeous backyard equipped with a pool, plenty of space to lounge, and a turf area where you could either practice your short game or play some other games. The ladies flew out of New Jersey Saturday morning on one of the casino's private jets. Once they touched down in Nevada, they were picked up by a stretch limo, courtesy of Sam, and brought to the villa.

"Ladies! Can I interest you all in some treats?" Sam exclaimed, giving the girls a grand welcoming. He held a silver tray with chocolate covered strawberries and held it out to them. They each took one and bit into them with a satisfying break into the chilled dark chocolate. "Come, follow me. There's so much more for you to see."

"You're looking amazing, Sam," one of the girls said. "Even better than when I saw you last."

"Aren't you a doll," Sam chuckled. "You can thank Dr. Ustafian for keeping me in tip-top shape for you girls."

"Mmm, I can see that," another lady chimed in, licking the strawberry juice from her lips.

"Champagne?" Sam led the ladies into the kitchen and pulled a bottle out from the ice bucket on the counter. The girls nodded with glee at being treated like queens as soon as they were in Sam's presence. "I hope you don't mind," he spoke as he poured, "but I pretty much have the whole day planned. As soon as you're all freshened up and settled in, I thought we'd get you girls to the spa while the guys and I hang out here. I'll have the car service pick you up whenever you're ready."

"Sounds wonderful," one said, taking her champagne and finishing it in one gulp.

They dropped their bags off before getting whisked away to the spa for some pampering. While they were away, the guys indulged in ESPN highlight reels and tanned by the pool. Once the girls came back, everyone got ready for a five-star dinner followed by partying at the club. Everything was VIP or else it was not even considered. The group was Vegas royalty, getting into places at the very last second and even let in late to a comedy show one of the guys felt like stopping into. They only stayed for twenty minutes before getting bored and moving on to something else. Eventually, they all made it back to their villa and commenced with some pillow talk. Sam had his girl picked for weeks, and she was ready to earn her keep.

The next day was Superbowl Sunday! Excitement was in the air as the gentleman placed bets on who they thought would come out on top. The televised halftime show, however, was not a topic of conversation. They had their own live halftime show scheduled for right out there on the putting green.

Each girl had a little case with her helmet, football jersey, long socks and thong inside. With three minutes left on the second quarter clock, they snuck off to get dressed. The men were screaming away at the television until the ladies walked back out, causing even more commotion. I can imagine how adorable they looked, with their knee socks pulled up high and their braided hair hanging down their backs from under their helmets. The ladies got in formation and hiked the ball, playing a skirmish as the guys cheered them on. They rolled around on the turf, tackling each other, and I was privy to receiving the occasional picture via text from Sam. I was almost a little jealous, it seemed like such a fun time! Playing went on for most of halftime until the girls were out of breath and all hot from their workout. They all stripped down and hopped in the pool, lounging until the game was over. The party continued into the evening, but it was spent at the villa with everyone drinking and canoodling, gazing off into the neon night. The Superbowl party was the envy of many of the girls on my roster and undoubtedly the next-door neighbors got an eyeful of the four hottest women in Vegas tackling each other.

Things died down slowly after February. Springtime wasn't a hugely busy time of year, but there was a notable uptick as the weather got warmer. I'd hear from Sam to schedule basic dates, but he had another big event for July Fourth weekend, which he'd host on his yacht in the Hamptons. The girls begged me to book them for it, not just because it was great money, but because it was a famously good time for everyone in attendance. It was hardly work for the girls who went, and I could feel their competitive spirits breaking through as May came to a close. They'd be sending me new photos, opening up their availability, and calling just to "say hi". I honestly enjoyed their efforts; it showed how hard-working they were and that they recognized a lucrative opportunity when it came around.

Sam was a lifelong bachelor, so there was no issue with the very public nature of this event. He'd, again, have four to six ladies booked for the weekend, all expenses paid. It was phenomenal because the ladies could just relax on the yacht once they arrived; Sam's only expectation for them was that they would be fun to be around. Luckily, I had plenty of stunners who knew how to treat a man to a good time!

Saturday was spent tanning and eating the finest food prepared by Sam's personal chef on board. You might think these rich blokes got bored, all that lounging and chatting, but Sam was someone who worked his butt off year-round; these events were the only long-term lounging he ever did. He took out the jet skis with his buddies, each with a girl holding tight behind him. As the sun set, they'd all get ready to stop by one or two of the famous Hampton parties, like the Carrots and Caviar party where the women dressed like *Playboy* bunnies and the men attempted to imitate Hef's nonchalant confidence. The ladies made sure they were prepared with various themed outfits to choose from because there were a lot of location changes and dress codes to adhere to. Even the clubs they went to had strict themes, many of them bordering on camp with their red, white, and blue suggestions for Independence Day weekend. Sam got everyone in with true VIP status, never waiting in one line or needing to call ahead, except maybe to make sure their drinks were ready as soon as they arrived. That status, and much more, was what made him such a desirable client.

For Sunday, things got started with a late brunch since everyone was sleeping in. Freshly squeezed juice was served, but not without champagne to complement it. I recall one time, during Sunday festivities, someone had brought Twister on board for everyone to play, but it wouldn't be just regular Twister. Cocaine was also involved; Sam like to partake but he wasn't a big user. The party got pretty wild, so I heard, and the Twister mat got doused with tanning oil. The ladies were slipping and falling all over each other, their skimpy bikinis barely holding them in. The oiled-up women shrieked with amusement as they fell, losing the game nearly all at once. Technically, there was no winner, but everyone felt like one, even those who weren't playing. It was rowdy and other boats passing by were endlessly interested in what Sam had going on. Anyone who was someone heard about Sam's great parties and tried to outdo him, but no one could even come close. He was too good at creating the atmosphere and for him, it was effortless. The women were gorgeous, the men were rich and sexy, and the Hamptons sun was shining bright. It was a fantasy I think many of us dream about.

The ladies usually left that trip with a small gift from Sam, as if the weekend itself wasn't enough. He had long-running arrangements with a few of my top girls; he wasn't someone who was constantly looking for someone new. One time, one of his favorites got a Rolex from him for her birthday, really drawing attention to how valuable a booking with Sam could be. He was, without a doubt, one of the most desirable bachelors I kept as a client. I can't thank him enough for how well he treated me and my girls.

# Tickle and Tease

A Madam's stories would be incomplete without including her tickle-obsessed clientele. It would be absolutely insane to not give you at least one (though there are so many more!). They are the easiest of clients, always more concerned with pleasure than pain, and the girls love them for it. How can you dislike a gent who comes to you to laugh, after all? I came across many in my day, but one stands alone due to the stark contrast between his professional and private life. He was a retired judge, presiding over felony cases in his day, but was the sweetest old man when he started booking through me. It was interesting, because he was very much still entwined with the legal scene in the city. He advised young lawyers and hosted dinners in his home. I didn't really view his kink as very controversial, but I suppose some in his circle might think otherwise. Luckily, his secret remains safe with me. I could never name names when it comes to the men who were nothing but good to me and my girls.

He called one afternoon as I sat down with a tea at my desk. The sunlight was peeking out from under the floral valence that hung from my office window, casting a glare across my computer screen.

"This is Anna, how can I help you?" I answered, feeling cheerful about the day ahead.

"It's good to hear your voice, dear. How are you?" the judge jumped right into friendly conversation. Back when memorizing numbers came a little easier to everyone, including myself, I could usually go without formal introductions for every call.

"Oh, you know, can't complain."

"That's good. Listen, have your read the *Times* today?"

"No, not yet. Anything good?"

"Meh, there's an exhibit opening up at The Met featuring some underground artist. Too modern for my tastes if you ask me."

"Oh, that's too bad."

"Well, I'll probably check it out anyway. Nothing better to do, I suppose."

"Would you like to bring along a plus one? Maybe a fresh set of eyes could help you enjoy it more," I said, leading him toward his true reason for calling.

"No, not this time. Just my usual room at the Carlyle if you could, for Saturday evening," he responded, sighing in the middle of his sentence.

"Of course," I said, picking up my tea, "and room service at the ready?"

"You know me too well. And who are you recommending?"

From the outside looking in, it appeared as if the judge was scheduling a romantic evening, perhaps celebrating an anniversary or birthday. But, no, such was not the case. For that particular evening, I booked him with Elisa after going through a few available ladies. Then I made the hotel reservations, specifying the champagne and desserts should be set up in the room before the guests arrived. A bouquet of flowers was also a requirement.

This preparation was the ambiance he required to feel comfortable in his innocently taboo exploit.

His fantasy was perfectly simple. On one of the many nights he booked with us, Elisa was set to arrive at the Carlyle at eight p.m. She'd be wearing a pearl encrusted hairclip, open-toed sandals with feathers or fur on the strap, and a silk nightie under her fur trench coat. In her purse, she'd bring along some props for the evening's escapade.

Inside the suite, the judge would be waiting to welcome Elisa with a grand spread of desserts, champagne on ice, and dimmed lights. Elisa took a moment to freshen up in the bathroom, unpacking her things and removing her coat. When she stepped out, she was Bette Davis born again, her deep blue eyes sending shivers up the judge's spine. They started with small talk over chocolate ganache cheesecake and glass after glass of bubbly. It truly sweetened the night and made both individuals comfy and close. Then, the teasing would begin.

Elisa had her share of titillating items set down beside her on the sofa, but the judge brought out a little red box for her to open.

"What's all this, Simon? A present?" she asked.

"It's for the both of us. For tonight," he smiled as she took from the box several red ribbons and large, white feathers. He continued, "You are in complete control, my dear. I'm at your mercy. If you wish to tie me up, so be it." Elisa was picking up on the hint, so she stood up, took the judge by the hand, and led him to a chair conspicuously placed in the center of the room. The judge, wearing his own tan silk robe, was seated once again, this time with his hands bound in red ribbon behind his back. Starting at his already curling toes, Elisa ever so gently skimmed the feather across his skin. It started with a smirk. Then, a giggle, until the judge was full belly laughing while Elisa touched every nook and cranny of the judge's body with the feather. His robe had parted, and Elisa could see his giddiness had risen him up considerably more than she thought the old man capable. It twitched as his grey-haired chest and belly button were tortured by Elisa's plumed prop. She rubbed her body against his, letting the nightie slip from her shoulders. He was in awe of her moonlit beauty and exposed his neck to her whims. It was a dance, a tease, and a joy for them both. Of course, this level of intimacy is hard to attain. That is why my services were so crucial. It allowed the touch-starved and power-stricken to let down their walls and allowed someone else, someone stunning and unjudgmental, to take the reins. After some time, he couldn't take it anymore. Elisa's sexy stalking around him and the teasing was racking through his body, and he begged to be untied. Elisa, seeing that it had gone on for plenty long, and knowing he might not be able to stay hard forever, untied him so he could gratify himself in the midst of a starlet. Odd, perhaps, but only to those on the outside of this industry. For us, this was as normal as normal could be.

# Pro Bono Bozo

Jason, a senior partner within a prestigious New York City law firm, called me for years without incident. Every week he booked an easy hour, always maintained a friendly rapport with the girls, and no one ever had any complaints about him.

Then, there was a sudden shift in Jason's behavior. I'm not sure what triggered it, but the beginning of the end all started with a stunning Canadian model who was in town for NY Fashion Week, making purchases for her personal collection and a co-owned boutique. She contacted me seeking out some quick cash so she could buy a little extra inventory for her store.

I sent her to Jason, relying on his dependability for a new girl. He left after fifteen minutes with her, time spent engaging in the full range of her services, chucking her a crumpled hundred-dollar bill on his way out the door. The girl was utterly confused at this short payment. I paid her the balance of her expected fee to keep the peace but called Jason first to hear his explanation.

"She just wasn't my type," he explained.

"I don't understand, Jay. She's a near spitting image of

Rebecca, and you went out with her for months. Something's changed?"

"Yeah, exactly. I don't want the same old thing all the time. It's boring."

"You should've said so earlier! I'm happy to hear about new tastes and preferences anytime, you know that."

"Just something interesting next time, okay?" and he hung up abruptly. I chalked it up to bad chemistry and didn't expect it to happen again. Although, his tone was rather off-putting.

Then we didn't hear from Jason for a few months in a row. He had never ghosted us like this, but I suppose that worked to his benefit because I didn't assume anything was wrong, necessarily. I simply believed he must've been too busy to book with us, perhaps due to a time-consuming case or promotion in his firm. I try always to assume the best in people, especially those I work for and with. It can certainly get me into trouble though like it did in this instance.

When Jason finally made a reappearance, it was in response to an ad I had placed for a lady named Martie, a model new to the city and trying to get her foot in the door. She had the warmest personality and was originally from the deep south. That accent was thicker than molasses and was a real turn-on for a lot of our clients.

I was looking forward to having Jason book with us again after he had been MIA for a while, but when the date went down, he left early once again and only paid $200, not even a fourth of Martie's full fee! I really couldn't have him booking girls for full-service hours just to leave them high and dry. I called to make my case, but only got his voicemail.

"Jason, it's Anna. This really isn't acceptable behavior. Now, we're happy to have you back, but you're treating these girls like trash. I understand both the girls you've ditched provided full service, but you're shorting them? You can either pay their full fees or pay nothing to receive nothing." I hoped my message was loud and clear, but apparently it did nothing but scare him off for a few more months before he came crawling back. But this time, I knew his MO. He wasn't about to take advantage of one of my girls again.

I was on a trip to Las Vegas when Jason popped back up, claiming a switch in firms had caused his sudden gap in bookings. My aunt had answered his call, reiterating to him that if he books with us, he'll now need to pay cash upfront because we couldn't risk his running off without paying again. He claimed to understand where we were coming from, so we gave him one more chance. After all, we had known him as a good client for years at that point. It seemed only cordial that we give him the benefit of the doubt. What a mistake that was.

Jason arrived at the booking, placing the girl's full fee on the table. She counted it, felt satisfied and comfortable, and they got to business. Forty hot and heavy minutes later, Jason washes up, grabs the money from the table, and goes to leave. When the girl snatched her money from him, money she had every right to take, he pushed her to the floor and grabbed it from her hand. Now, he had shown his true colors to me. Abuse towards the girls is *never* tolerated. The very few times things have escalated on account of a client's violence, it results in immediate blacklisting.

My aunt called me in Las Vegas and told me what had transpired. I was infuriated that a client was not only exploiting my trust but had now acted outwardly abusive towards a respectable working girl. It didn't matter that I was away from the office; in fact, that made the offense even more repulsive. He probably thought my absence would allow him to get away with it. He had no idea what he had gotten himself into. I asked my aunt to pass along this message from me, for Jason: If he didn't pay every penny required to the girl who had just serviced him by six p.m. that night, things would not end well for him. He had my word.

My aunt, in her very proper English accent, gave him my

message in a calm and assertive tone. He responded by kindly asking her to fuck off because we weren't going to be able to touch him. Now he had really done himself in, disrespecting my family after all the bullshit he had been pulling. He thought that his little change in employer would keep me from being able to contact his new firm, but he should've known I was better at keeping tabs on clients than the freakin' government. It was my job, after all, to know what they were up to and provide for them accordingly. My aunt sent me his cell and office number and I gave Jason a warning call. It was of no consequence to me that he didn't answer; my voicemail was loud and clear. I simply let him know that if I wasn't able to get ahold of him in the next hour or so, I'd have to make a call to his law firm, which might make things somewhat awkward for him. Well, not ten minutes went by before his number illuminated my caller ID and the conversation that followed was colorful, to say the least. I recall it rather vividly.

"Jason, hello. So glad you called back," I started.

"Listen here, you fucking bitch. I'll blow the cover on your whole illegal operation if you so much as type the office number into your phone."

"Let me be blunt. I have nothing to lose. I'm an uneducated 'hooker booker' and I don't have a pot to piss in. I believe I'm right in saying your degree, your wife and child, and your career are all on the line. So, how's about you pay your fee?"

His continued cursing and yelling were really starting to piss me off. I told him that because of his stubbornness, I'd have to take an earlier flight back to the city and I was tacking that cost onto his outstanding fee. Then I hung up.

Just to make things a little more real for him, I left a message on his new office answering machine. I let him know that when I land, around seven in the morning, I might just swing by his office with donuts and coffee for him and his coworkers. I hoped that might sweeten things when I deliver the bitter news about his despicable stumble into abusing women and that maybe a larger caseload would keep him from doing it again, especially during company hours.

By the time I landed in Newark, I had a dozen or more messages from Jason, begging me to relent. He promised to pay double the outstanding fee if I gave him a location to drop it off. I didn't respond, because if men like him had any sense, he would've known that it wasn't about the money anymore. He lost that chance way before I got on my returning flight. It was about his behavior, his entire outlook on how working women should be treated. It was horrific that during the time I was operating my business, women were still totally at risk of violence by the men they should have been able to trust. It should have been a symbiotic relationship. Instead, he was one of those predators who are only interested in sex if it is toxic in nature. I couldn't tolerate it and everything about the way I did business was an attempt to protect my employees from these types of people. True scum of the earth, they are. My threats about going to his office were, unfortunately, empty; I couldn't risk publicly humiliating him because he really did have more leverage than I. But at least it worked in getting the message across.

I couldn't take his incessant calling any longer. It wasn't allowing for any other calls to come through, so I finally answered him and said, "I'm in New York on my way to your office. Where's the nearest Dunkin' and what kind of donuts do you like best? It's on me." He pleaded with me, asking to meet so he could pay the fee, double if I wanted it. I replied, "You'll pay the added $100 for my flight change, and you'll tip the girl no less than $50 on top of her fee because of how you treated her." He agreed and, within 20 minutes, he paid her the full fee plus the additional $50 for his bad behavior.

I called him after the money was dropped off and said, "Thank you for doing the right thing, but I think I need to clarify that you are no longer welcome to call again. If you try to call under an assumed name, and I figure it out, I will be your worst nightmare." I never heard from him again.

A few months later, I learned he called another service and hit the girl, leaving her with a bad concussion. He had found a new hunting ground on a sugar daddy dating site, which I am sure he was using to find innocent women to prey upon. Ladies, he is still out there and claims to be an attorney in NYC. His name is Jason B. If you're a working girl, stay safe out there.

# Murder Mystery Weekend

When ski season came around on the east coast, Steven (yes, that Steven) would book a few ladies for a winter-weather trip. One year it was the Poconos, another was spent in New Hampshire. Oftentimes, though, he chose an upscale ski lodge in Vermont, where he rented a large private cabin. Coincidentally, his birthday was around the same time as this yearly trip, and he threw a whole separate event for that. This trip was just a fun adventure Steven liked to host that included a few of his personal friends and a handful of my top girls, with his birthday being the cherry on top.

The cabin was nestled into the pine trees and certainly boasted a remote locale for weekend getaways. The weekend I'm musing on here started out as a pain in the butt, and it came to be the last ski weekend trip I ever booked with Steven. There was a huge blizzard, multiple feet of snow slowing travel down for everyone invited, but especially the girls I was sending. They were stuck behind plows for seven hours because they had been told to arrive a day later than everyone else. It was a nightmare! Before they even arrived at the cabin, they were going stir-crazy. I can't even remember how many texts I got from each of them saying that if I ever required them to go to Vermont in January again, their rate would be tripled for the sheer hassle it was to get there. Can't say I blame them.

They were supposed to arrive at noon, but the ladies crossed the threshold of this massive lodge in the peaks of Vermont around half-past seven. A gentleman with a pencil-thin mustache donning coattails welcomed them with a blood orange cocktail served from a silver platter. There were seven bedrooms and a jacuzzi that could comfortably fit ten to twelve people. Each of my four ladies was given her own room, told to unpack, freshen up, and return to the main hall for dinner in an hour. When the dinner bell rang, everyone strolled into the hall and found they had been assigned a seat, alternating between the men and women present. Steven's guests, his friends, and a few other ladies were dressed in 1920s style, while a butler presided over the meal. He announced the plans for the trip; it was to be a murder mystery-themed weekend in celebration of Steven's birthday. A round of applause erupted from the guests, though my girls were somewhat in the dark about what would be expected of them. Luckily, the host had brought a trunk filled to the brim with spare vintage costumes for the girls to change into. They each did so, but not before calling me as a group and asking for advice.

"Did Steven mention that this was going to be, like, a big, themed thing?" one of my girls called and asked.

"No, he didn't, though I wish he had," I told her.

"What should we do?"

"I guess just try to go with the flow. If anything seems to be getting out of hand, just call," I said, wishing I had better advice than I did. Unfortunately, I had nothing more helpful to say. The best I could do was wish them luck and hope it ended up being a fun time for them! It's too bad that only some of the partiers were to enjoy themselves that trip.

Dinner commenced when the ladies returned, where four

indulgent courses were served one after the other. The girls came to understand that some of the guests were actually actors involved in the creation of a believable and immersive scene. One of the actors would disappear from the group and be the "victim", while the rest of the party attempted to figure out who the murderer was. After dinner, the crime was committed. The victim was found bleeding, a corn syrup mixture pooling about his head, and a broken lamp seemed to be the murder weapon. Now, it was a race against the clock to discover the murderer before they could strike again! There was one more twist though; unbeknownst to Steven's regular guests and the actors, my ladies were there for the inevitable sexual relief required when hunting a killer. All that adrenaline can really go to your pants, and, for that, the ladies needed no advice from me.

As the cast members were trying to perform the investigation portion of the night, Steven and his friends got their hands on my girls, leading them to the jacuzzi stark naked. Once again, out came the party goods and the night went off the rails from there. Bumps of coke were had by all, snorted from that same silver platter the actor-butler had used to serve drinks earlier in the night. The high and drunk revelers attempted to continue playing the game and help the actors collect clues, but eight under the influence guests do not effective detectives make. It was like wrangling greased pigs. At one point, one of the actresses was attempting to find Steven so he could read the next clue to every-one, but she walked in and saw Elisa spanking him with a leather crop while he wore nothing but bowler hat. Elisa, embarrassed by the intrusion, stormed out of the room, her tiered evening gown tripping her on the way out.

Things continued to devolve. One of my girls, Kiki, drunk as a skunk, got offended by something someone said. In the middle of a snowstorm, where accumulation had already hit the three-foot marker, she walked out the front door wearing a flapper costume and five-inch heeled boots. Not for one second would anyone with their senses about them think she was dressed appropriately for the weather. Quite the opposite was true, in fact. The partiers were yelling at her to come back inside or else she'd get hypothermia or frostbite. After much persuasion, once the windchill had hit her right in the bones, Kiki went back in and shivered her way up the stairs to her room, saying nothing to everyone as she passed them.

The rest of the night was basically an orgy that could've rivaled any rock star's sexual debauchery. Some of Steven's friends even tried to get the actresses to join in, only to be met with vehement declinations. They never did figure out who the killer was and to this day it remains an unsolved mystery. In the morning, the actors left without so much as a goodbye. I do hope they were paid handsomely to put up with Steven's bad behavior.

It was a weekend the girls talked about for months after it ended. The sheer insanity of actors attempting to play out a scene with a group of partiers who could hardly walk a straight line never failed to get a good laugh from us all. It was the first and last X-rated murder mystery party my girls ever attended.

A few months later, Steven called to let me know he had rented a space of some sort in Las Vegas and was wondering if I could hook him up with a dominatrix for a couple of days. No problem there, of course, as I had multiple dommes on my roster. She was told to pick up keys for the rental and wait for a delivery. When the shipment arrived, it was a large coffin-sized box nailed shut. The domme was completely confused but waited for Steven to arrive, which he did shortly following the delivery. He opened the box and it contained planks of wood and power tools. My domme swiftly left the place, feeling utterly unsafe by what she saw. Turns out, Steven booked the rental because it was large enough for him to construct a wooden cross, which he wished to be strung up to and tortured for days on end. It was a dark path that he was going down, and I stopped booking with him after that. One more lunatic I had to kick to the curb, unfortunately.

# Bus Stop Bill

People like to assume that every aspect of my job, the industry I worked in, was some sinful exploit, an entirely evil operation. It isn't true, naturally, but people like to criticize what they do not understand, especially when it comes to women maintaining authority over their own bodies. They were the masters of their own lives and were paid handsomely for the services they provided. The ladies under my employ were regularly dealing with the men who held sway over political or financial decisions that impacted hundreds of lives or more. Others were just regular men. In that mix, one could find that there was an iota of individuals who could be considered a dark soul. It wouldn't be honest if I didn't include at least one such person who did make my skin crawl a bit.

This man was a client of our in-call house, where different ladies were on staff depending on the day, performing services in the various rooms within. When a man arrived for an appointment, the girls would all come through and introduce themselves. Then the client could pick out whichever girl catches his eye. There was a regular, Bill, who came by on Tuesdays at 5:30

p.m. He went right to his usual room, room 3, and waited for the girls to make their appearance. One such Tuesday, he chose Carrie, a nineteen-year-old new to the industry. He handed her a bag containing a short plaid skirt, white blouse, and knee socks. He asked that she get dressed and preferred if she could wear flat shoes once she came back.

In each parlor room, there is a massage table, a coat stand, a chair, and a small vanity filled with baby oil, powder, and tissues. Simplistic, but it served its purpose swimmingly for every client. When Carrie came back to the room, dressed in her uniform, Bill's clothes were piled on the chair and he was sitting on the massage table, a long trench coat closed around him, and he was pretending to drive a vehicle. A brown paper bag was on the table next to him. I'm not sure how she didn't burst out laughing at the sight, but she was good at her job from the start. The phone booker had given her the script Bill provided before she went in. She went and stood by the coat stand, pretending to wait for the bus. Bill made sputtering engine noises as he pretended to pull his car up to the stop.

"Little girl," Bill said, "do you need a ride?"

"My mom told me not to talk to strangers," Carrie replied staunchly.

"But I work for the church, and you look so cold standing out here all alone. I can help take you home to your mommy."

"Mommy said I shouldn't get in a stranger's car."

"Mommy is teaching you to be very smart. I have a treat for smart little girls like you."

"You do? What kind of treat?" Carrie said, stepping towards the imaginary car window.

"Come see," Bill said, crinkling the paper bag and shaking its contents. Carrie leaned over him and looked into the bag. It was filled with lollipops. "What flavor do you like?"

"Hmm, cherry!" Carrie said excitedly. Bill pulled out a

cherry lollipop and handed it to her. She popped it into her mouth, making small sucking sounds and smiling.

"I'm Bill. What's your name, little one?"

"Carrie," Carrie said.

"Now we aren't strangers, are we? Why don't you come sit in the passenger seat and I'll get you home? You can even have another sucker if you want!" Bill patted the table beside him and Carrie walked around to sit. He asked her about school and what she liked to do in her free time, what games she liked to play. Carrie swung her feet as she spoke, looking all around her as she finished her lollipop. When she was done, she asked if she could have another.

"Of course you can, princess. You can have as many as you like, but I have a special sucker, but you have to promise me we're friends first," Bill said.

"Yeah, we're friends, I promise! I want the special one," Carrie said. When she promised, Bill opened up his coat to reveal a raging hard-on. He grabbed Carrie's hand and put it on his boner.

"That's a weird lolly, mister. I think mommy is going to be mad at me if I touch that," Carrie said, pulling her hand away. Bill loved to hear this part of the script and he finished himself off in no time. She needn't touch him very much for his fantasy to be fulfilled, as it was all imagination and scene setting. Carrie grabbed a wet towel from another room and wiped Bill off. They talked a little while he got dressed and he put the money on the vanity before he left. Once he was gone, she changed the sheets to prepare for the next john.

We were an outlet, a better resort, for people who otherwise might've sought out predation or other unsavory activities. I would rather provide this service a million times over than have any child subjected to danger. I understand that this can be difficult to reconcile with; I feel the same way. I could never know how these men where operating outside my parlor doors; the truth is, you never know, can never suspect who among us is thinking these revolting thoughts. There is a dark side to every industry; everything has pros and cons. And with youthfulness being touted as synonymous with beauty, one might want to look to what our society promotes as "sexy" when pondering the root cause of this fantasy.

# Saran Wrap Man

My career as a madam redefined what I thought of as "odd." When fantasies pop into men's heads, they don't only remain there for a long time; they often become more sensational and peculiar. Those with the audacity to act things out came to me, and I provided the experience of a lifetime for them. Workingwomen all over the world will tell you there isn't a fetish that could surprise them. All in a day's work, they would say. A client could have come in requesting a woman with two heads and I wouldn't have thought much of it. There was no way to predict what new and spectacular request would slip through the lips of men on the other end of the phone line. Although I will say, I think some of these men need a shrink, not a madam. But I did what I could and there's no shame in it, even when it came to an end.

Jeff was a freak, no question about it, but generally harmless. He just had some quirks that some girls found a bit off-putting. His paranoia caused him to believe we were spying on him, so he always preferred to choose the location for his bookings. There was this one occasion where the location he chose was actually a very public, very busy nail salon owned by a friend of his. You can imagine my girl's discomfort as she led a chubby, Hasidic man into the waxing room at the back of the salon, the eyes of every patron and nail tech upon them.

Jeff went through an interesting phase for a few months. He booked a girl and asked that she bring six rolls of saran wrap and candles with her to the hotel room he was renting. I didn't ask him what they were for; I didn't really want to know. Of course, I found out later when the girl he booked told me about it, barely able to get the words out as she giggled. Jeff let the girl in and immediately stripped down to his birthday suit. He instructed her to swaddle him in the saran wrap, leaving only two gaps in the layers: a gap for his mouth and one for his penis. It took a while, but soon enough he was enveloped in what must've been about an inch and a half of plastic. Then, she sealed the wrap with melted wax from the candles.

"You're a gross little man," she said, following his deprecating script. "You don't deserve pleasure."

"Please, please mistress," he begged. "I know I'm bad, but please, I'll do anything." Jeff was gasping between breaths, his mouth forced to choose between words and oxygen.

"Anything?" mistress asks. "How about you roll around on the floor, worm," she demanded. This scenario was a first for her, but she clearly took it in stride! Jeff flopped onto the carpet with a thud, squirming helplessly. He begged for a hand job and got it, soon enough. He ejaculated on the floor beside him and then the girl cut him free of his unnatural cocoon. He dressed, paid her fee, and they went their separate ways. He was not totally satiated by this hour-long session.

The next time, he wanted a new girl at a new location. When the girl, Emma, arrived, she was hesitant because the address brought her to a dance studio, the parking lot full of minivans and SUVs. She called to voice her concerns and I connected with Jeff about the issue.

"What's all this about the dance studio, Jeff? I don't recall seeing anything about a studio under your ownership in your profile. Are you risking my girl's safety with some kind of secret public stunt?"

"I would never! Have a little faith, why don't ya. My friend owns the studio, not me, but he has a very private space in the back that is never used by employees or anyone. Only he has access to it, and he gave me a key 'cuz he knows what I'm about. Nothing could possibly go wrong, I promise!" he pleaded.

"Don't bullshit me, Jeff. You've been a little out of pocket lately," I said as I drummed my fingers across my lap.

"I swear to God, Anna, no bullshit."

"Alright, fine. I'll let your girl know," and hung up to call Emma back. After she was assured everything was on the up and up, she walked in and asked for Jeff. She was directed back to the office, which was actually an unused studio room, the floor to ceiling wall of mirrors throwing midday sun across the light wood flooring. Jeff was already seated, in the nude, in the center of the room. He was saran wrapped to the chair, the two gaps left again for pleasure and instructions. He asked Emma to melt candle wax onto the tip of his erection. By the fourth or fifth drop of hot wax, he finished without even being touched by Emma. She said it was the easiest, but perhaps weirdest, $1,000 she ever made. I wonder if that remains true to this day.

Freaky Jeff was really stuck on this saran wrap skit! He called a few weeks after booking Emma and asked for someone new to the business, a fresh face so to speak. He wanted there to be some shock factor when he introduced her to his restrictive kink. He told me she must come in business attire, with her briefcase stocked with the necessary materials discreetly hidden within. He gave me an address for the meeting: an office on the fortieth floor of the Empire State Building. This date was sure to be an interesting introduction into the world of escorting for my bright-eyed and bushy-tailed newcomer.

Meg adjusted her fitted blazer and pulled up her tights as she rode the elevator up to the office. Once she located it, she walked up to two women sorting various-sized diamonds and ring bands behind a brightly lit counter.

"Hello, I'm here to see Mr. Berger for a meeting," she said to the women, who looked at her with clear disdain. However, one lady did come from behind the counter to lead Meg through a door off to the side of the room. She closed the door behind Meg, leaving her in the room alone. Jeff arrived after her, a few minutes late for his appointment, so they began right away. Wrapped and wax sealed, he finished in minutes, grunting loudly enough that the ladies in the room over were surely able to hear him. Meg was beet red as she exited, confronted with looks of disgust from the diamond dealer employees and gentleman there to pick out an engagement ring. She rushed out the doors as fast as her stockinged legs would carry her.

It wasn't the action, but the public nature of the meetings, that was making things difficult between us and Jeff. Voyeurism is common, but matched with Jeff's kink, it was too risky. I stopped booking him unless he agreed to conduct his business in a hotel room or apartment. God forbid someone were to walk in on them at one of these very public places; my girl would definitely ditch Jeff to protect herself. Then we'd have another "Pigs in a Blanket" situation on our hands! Even though I think it stressed him out a little and he ended up conducting a top-to-bottom search of every room he booked, it was a lot less risky than the offices he preferred. We found a happy medium, in my opinion!

# Playing with Dolls

Alberto had a very particular type when it came to women. He liked them very petite, slim, no taller than five feet one inch tall, and wrinkle-free. Now, this was not my typical girl. Most of the women on my roster were big girls, full-figured and tall. I told Alberto that I'd have to call around and get back to him. I assumed he might've been a shorter man, so he was looking for a petite woman to make him feel very strong and masculine. I wasn't exactly hitting the mark with that assumption.

I asked a colleague for help, and she referred me to a few different women to check in with. The first was Sandra, a real estate agent from Miami who dabbled in the industry on the side when sales were slow. She was perfect, only five feet tall, but she didn't want to travel all the way to the city for work. Moving on, I called a woman named Josefina. Her thick accent was very difficult to understand, but something I would normally look past. Unfortunately, she was way too tall even if she was petite otherwise. I also called a woman named Stacey, whose coldness was immediately apparent on the call. I saw her headshots and she was stunningly beautiful and small, but an icy attitude is never good for business. Women like that have a hard time keeping a client happy because there's not even an attempt at making a connection. I was getting discouraged after interviewing so many people, I wasn't sure I'd be able to find someone fast enough.

Then, like a blessing, Helena came into my life looking for work. She was a gorgeous Australian with a Grace Kelly vibe. I wasn't sure if I could give her a lot of work for the short time she'd be in New York, but I was feeling pretty confident about matching her with Alberto. I told her I'd try to find her a few appointments, but luckily, she was thrilled about even getting one booking. I sent Alberto her photos and he enthusiastically booked her right away. He specified that she should arrive for their date without wearing any makeup or nail polish on her fingers or toes. Still befuddled about what his special interest might be, I made the arrangements and gave Helena Alberto's address before she made her way there.

He lived alone in a brownstone on the Upper West Side, right near Central Park. I'm sure the price tag on such a home was lofty. He was referred to me by a friend of similar status, so he had a little bit of leeway in being allowed to have a woman over to his house for his first booking. Money and connection never equal trustworthy, though, so I made sure our security staff was on high alert in case things went south. For new clients, security operated on an on-call basis for an extra measure of safety. Helena used the large brass knocker to announce her arrival. Alberto answered the door with drinks in hand and led his tiny lady into an enormous living room, fashioned with a grand piano in the corner and picture windows overlooking his garden in the backyard. A live-in butler came to refill their glasses with Sloan Estate red wine, coming in at around $800 for that particular bottle. After they were topped off, Alberto dismissed his butler for the night.

They ate a scrumptious dinner and chatted amicably. Alberto

said, "I hope you don't mind, but after dinner I'd love to show you a very special place in my home. A collection of mine, if you will. I have very exciting plans for the evening."

"I'd love to see," Helena said, nodding and smiling. "Sounds like fun."

They walked hand in hand up a wide staircase with an intricately carved banister and moved down the hall of the second floor. Helena expressed to me after the fact that even though they were alone, she felt completely at ease. There was something about Alberto that made her feel like he was innocent. She must've had some reliable intuition, that Aussie. Alberto fumbled momentarily with a key, then successfully unlocked the door to his secret room. Helena gasped in amazement at what she saw.

The room was filled with long lines of clothing racks filled with dresses in every hue imaginable. Pastel pinks and greens were set beside bright blues and buttercream yellows. The wallpaper was antique, a playful display of nymphs and centaurs frolicking in open fields. The only interruption to the scene were various mirrors set up against the walls, with gilded gold frames. On one end of the room was a plush deep-red velvet sofa, matching the thick velvet curtains that went the length of the entire windowed wall. Against the adjacent wall, a large vanity befitting a Broadway star illuminated the space around it with a warm light. Finally, in the corner, a huge, white, clawfoot bathtub sat surrounded by luxurious ottomans and shelves laden with bath salts and flowery essential oils.

This was Alberto's secluded wonderland.

He handed Helena a cream-colored chenille bathrobe and asked her to get comfortable as he began to run the bathwater, asking her what type of salts she preferred. She settled on lemongrass. She slipped into the lusciously scented water and Alberto placed a feather-soft towel on the back of the tub to cradle her neck. He then took a thick white loofah and began to wash her, starting with her legs, moving up her entire body, and humming as he did. When he finished, he helped her to step out of the bath and slowly examined every inch of her, complimenting her as he placed her robe back on.

"My pet, you are flawless. So little," he cooed in her ear. Small in stature as she was, her hips were full, and Alberta rested his large hand at the crook of her waist where the thin belt brought the fabric up against her. He had to bend a good deal down to speak to her in whispers. He knelt behind her then, his head level with her shoulder blades, and lifted the robe just so the curve of her pert bottom was revealed. Losing his breath with each additional inch of skin exposed, he felt like rushing ahead. Never before had a woman fit his fantasy so precisely, so effort-lessly. But he knew he'd be kicking himself if he did not indulge in every course. He planted a firm, sucking kiss at the small of her back before letting the robe recover its place over her behind.

"I don't think I've ever-" Helena began to say.

"No, sweet one. You need no words. Your beauty speaks volumes."

They walked to the vanity then, but Alberto had her face away from the mirror. He rifled through shelves of color-coordi-nated makeup palettes. Not drugstore brands either. Urban Decay, Lancôme, and Charlotte Tilbury were smattered about, clearly well used. Such an array was more than celebrity makeup artists kept in their arsenal.

"Sit, please. I've always loved makeup, even when I was a little boy. Made my father rather angry, but I was never a fruit. I would do my mother's makeup as often as she allowed it because she was so beautiful, and I wanted to make her even more so. Now, it would be an honor to do the same for you." He kissed her arms and fingers, making wet little noises with his lips as he spoke against her skin. It gave her goosebumps.

She, of course, accepted his offer. If he were to use every type of product he had available, she'd be there for hours, and she saw dollar signs floating about her head. He was already a high-paying client at $1,500 an hour. She hoped he'd take his time.

He custom-mixed her foundation to match her skin tone perfectly, applying it with a damp sponge. Then came gentle contouring, eyeshadow, lashes, liner, and pink blush on the apples of her cheeks. He saved lipstick for last, but she couldn't look at his mastery quite yet. He skipped over to a vintage Louis Vuitton trunk. Held within were multiple satin bags containing human hair wigs of various sizes, colors, and textures. He picked out a long brunette piece and covered Helena's blonde hair with it. He plugged in a curling iron and styled the wig to have big, bouncy curls framing Helena's face. A box was placed at the back of her head, but it was large enough to see it from the front.

Next came dress-up. He picked out thigh-high white stockings and gently rolled them up over her knees. He had her stand while he adjusted them, making sure the seam up the back was perfectly straight. Alberto stood discriminately before his racks of clothing before settling on a frilly Shirley Temple style dress. It was the color of lemonade. All of the clothes were securely zippered within clear plastic drycleaner's bags. He pulled it out and fluffed it by carefully shaking it about. Helena had great intuition, as I mentioned, but it took her a minute to figure out what was going on. The lightbulb went off, though, and she delicately looked up at Alberto.

"Am I your little doll?" she asked. He nodded, pleased with her discovery. He held the dress open at her feet so she could step into it, then he zipped her up.

Finally, Helena was allowed to see herself. It was unlike anything she had ever seen. She was like one of those Victorian porcelain dolls that have been standing in little girls' rooms for decades, never aging or changing. The lace collar of her dress elongated her neck in an elegant and flattering way, but the rest of the dress hid her body such that she was bordering on frumpiness. Alberto stood behind her, his hands on her dainty shoulders, admiring his work. She could see he was undressing then, and she turned to face him, twirling her hair as she smiled. He reached out to touch her frills, stepping close to her and smelling her flowery skin. Alberto put on some soft, lullaby style music and asked Helena to walk around and bend over in front of him, becoming erect from simply watching his live doll in action. They sat together on the sofa, Alberto touching himself until his loud grunt of pleasure erupted from him. He lost his composure only briefly before returning to his normal self.

"Thank you so much. You are divine. May I take a few photos, for my personal use?" he asked. "I'll give you an extra thousand for just three pictures." Helena had hit the jackpot with Alberto. She wouldn't have made this much if I had been able to book her with three other clients that week! Alberto posed her on the velvet couch, opening the curtains very slightly so the moonlight could play in her hair and reflect off her pale skin.

"He might have a crazy fetish," she told me afterward, "but he was so sweet and considerate and generous, I really didn't mind him at all."

Alberto became a long-time regular, resulting in a large collection of photo albums documenting his decadent dress-up sessions. He'd be able to relive those moments long after they came to a close and, for him, that was priceless. I found myself constantly seeking out tiny models for him at least once a month, and we all made great money when he called.

# Tales from the Crypt

My most memorable john was Vincent, The Count, a very old man who I started booking when he was already eighty-something years old. I booked him right through to his mid-nineties, go figure. He was a famous horror movie director in the 1960s and 70s, and I'm sure everyone reading has seen or heard of at least one of his films. Perhaps I'm dating myself. Seems like only yesterday we were all experiencing that nostalgic age of media. I'm not sure we've truly made improvements other than graphic quality. But I digress. Every Thursday night he'd call, looking for a fresh set of legs for the scene he'd set week after week.

All the girls knew about The Count and his crazy plot. They'd laugh and tease whenever he chose his next victim, knowing what she'd be in for. One week, he booked Helena, that twenty-three-year-old from Australia who was new to the roster. The girls kept the script a secret from her, almost using The Count as a way to haze the new girl. Not to worry, though, because I prepped her for the events to come.

"He's really nothing to be worried about. The girls are just teasing you," I told her while we sat in a café to discuss the arrangement. She was sitting with the window behind her, the sun casting shadows across the table between us. She stirred her drink by moving it in small, circular motions upon the tabletop.

"I'm not really worried about the date. I feel like he's such a big client and I'm not really qualified. This will only be my second time."

"If I could, I'd have every new girl go to Vincent. It's going to be such easy money, you'll feel like you're stealing." She sighed somewhat heavily. "If you don't want to, though, that's not a problem! I just thought you'd be interested."

"No, I am! Just nerves, I guess," she said with a puckered face.

"You'll be great. Make sure you have a bit of tea with honey beforehand. Keep that throat lubricated," I said. She laughed at that, and I knew Vincent would be a very happy customer.

In all honesty, I was surprised Helena hadn't heard about him yet; he was by far the most legendary john in New York, thanks to his advanced age and longevity in seeking out escort services. And I was the lucky lady who served him for nearly a decade. I know plenty of other madams who wished they hooked him the way I had. Of course, Helena had come from out of state and was learning as she went.

Ivan, the creepy lurch that manned Vincent's door, let Helena in at precisely nine o'clock after she'd been driven in by one of Vincent's personal drivers. She walked up the steep stone steps to a towering front door. Ivan was a six-and-a-half-foot tall ghostly man who, I assume, was one of the only people Vincent trusted with knowing all that went on in his multimillion-dollar Upper East Side brownstone. He greeted her with an eerie "good evening" and led her inside. Celebrities and millionaires lined the entire block, but they were none the wiser about Vincent's activities, although there were rumors. Helena had reviewed the script and was ready to act her little heart out.

Ivan brought her to a door leading into the basement, and that was where his duty ended for the time being. Carefully displayed throughout this lower level were original props from various classic horror films, *The Mummy*, *Dracula*, and *Frankenstein*, to name a few. The hallway was lit with candelabras mounted upon the walls, flickering shadows upon framed black and white movie posters. Movie theater-style floor lights directed Helena down the hall, and she began to call out into the dimness.

"Hello? Is anyone here?" she yelled, moving slowly through the hall and into a large room. There were life-sized figurines and props all over the room. She wandered around, taking in each of the horrifying masks and razor-sharp cleavers on display. Being so young, and also not from America, she was unfamiliar with a lot of the movies featured, and she made a mental note to look into them. She was a big fan of horror movies from the 90s, so maybe she'd like these old classics, she thought. She got so distracted inspecting all the props, she nearly forgot what she was there to do. Refocusing, she spun around and took in the behemoth sight. In the middle of the room, set upon a raised space, was a huge, closed coffin, illuminated by four candle stands placed at each corner.

"Hello? Is there somebody here?" Helena said, her voice shaking. From within the coffin, she could hear what she thought was breathing, low and raspy. She walked up to it slowly, making as if she was going to open it. She stood there with her hand hovering for many seconds, forcing her breath to become labored. Then, she flung the cover open and brought her hands to her face in convincing fear, screaming at the top of her lungs.

Vincent sat up with a start, stark naked except for an open cloak and Dracula fangs in his mouth, reeling toward her from his place in the coffin. He reached for her with one wrinkly hand while he jerked his wimpy erection with the other. She ran from his grasp as fast as she could, stumbling in the dark, screaming all the while. When she made it to the front door, Ivan held out her envelope and opened the door for her in one movement. The limo was waiting for her on the street. She was just like the girls in the movies, running for her life when the monster appeared.

The whole thing took no longer than fifteen minutes from arrival, usually less than ten. One might think that Vincent would only agree to pay the minimum then since so little time was spent, and he barely even saw the girl. But it was the screaming that got him going. The supposed fear coursing through her was the very thing that made his night each week. He had the entire place soundproofed so he could get the loudest lungs he could get, and no one would hear a thing, except for him and Ivan. He usually liked new faces, but he booked an opera singer I had on my roster multiple times in a row whenever he couldn't find a new face he liked. It was a special talent, that blood-curdling sound, and he paid premium fees for the right screech. Typically, for his ten-minute booking, he paid no less than $3,000. He paid even more if it was Halloween time. All October long, he paid upwards of $5,000 just for a woman to open her mouth and shriek like a tea kettle. Like I said, my girls and I were lucky he was such a consistent patron.

# Death of a Billionaire Queen

The sound of the VIP line ringing was exhilarating. The clients that called through were our big hitters; multi-millionaires and billionaires with nothing but money and power to spare. One could rely on them to book two girls or more nearly every time they called, and they were never just booking a room. No, these gentlemen were taking girls on international trips, week-long getaways, and parties where you might run into A-list celebrities. For them, I kept a roster of exclusive girls who knew exactly how to keep these gents entertained. It was a list only I had access to, and frequently the girls on it got used to be booked only with these types of clients. It was almost like a separate sect of the business.

The line rang one sunny Thursday afternoon, and it was Byron, a famous online gaming billionaire in his early thirties. His 590-foot-long yacht had just dropped anchor at the port of Ibiza, but he was feeling lonely. He wanted to fly out three ladies for a few days of company, ladies who were at least six foot five, as he was a rather tall man himself. Normally, I'd be against an international trip with a client with a well-known cocaine habit, but Byron was always the impeccable gentleman and never pushed his use on my girls, so I entertained the booking. After ten minutes of running through the available talent, though I intentionally left out a couple of girls who were known to get rowdy, Byron selected three tall beauties: April and Chloe who were British models, and Svetlana, a Russian model who often worked out of Paris in runway shows. Byron gave me his credit card information so we could take care of arranging the girls' travel and pay their fees in advance.

As it was my strict policy to have my girls call in upon arrival, each of them did so, agog at how luxurious the yacht was. On-board staff attended to everything the girls needed and made them aware of the proposed itinerary for the time that they'd be accompanying Byron. First order of business was stripping down to just their bikini bottoms and hitting the deck for some sun and cocktails. The girls spread out on various cushioned lounge chairs, sipping mango daiquiris while Byron stopped for a chat with each of them. He danced between the chairs in his barely-there speedo, twirling in the sunlight. He was up in the clouds and had probably been there since he docked. He had no plans of coming back down to earth.

I heard nothing but short affirmations of smooth sailing for nearly three days. Then, my phone rang in the middle of the night. I felt it in my stomach that something bad had happened even before I snatched the phone up and heard April, crying hysterically, on the other end.

"Calm down, honey," I told her. "Take a few deep breaths. Now, tell me you're okay."

"I'm fine," she quickly replied. "It's not me! It's Byron! He's not moving and there's white foam coming out of his mouth!" My heart sank. This was bad. Worse than bad.

"Where are Chloe and Svetlana?" I asked.

"Chloe's sleeping and Svetlana locked herself in her room."

"Well, what happened!"

"We had finished an early dinner in the main dining room

when he took us to the living room. There was this huge brick of cocaine on a coffee table," she explained. "Then he asked us to get the shaving kit in the master bathroom. He was snorting line after line the whole time we shaved his legs and his chest and his face. He told Svetlana to get his suitcase from his bedroom, and when she opened it up, we all saw the piles of makeup. And some stockings and shoes and wigs."

The girls didn't have to be rocket scientists to know exactly what this night's gig was going to be about. Especially when the shoes were a men's size 13.

"Chloe was in charge of doing his makeup," April went on, "while me and Svetlana started rolling up his stockings. He was so tall they wouldn't go any higher than his knees! We put a long black wig on him and helped him into a pair of red heels. He was prancing around the room and asking us how pretty he was, and of course we told him he was so gorgeous and so hot, and his body was so sexy. And then he asked Svetlana to open a cabinet behind the sofa and hand him a crack pipe." She started to cry. "That's when everything started to go all bugger-up. He was smoking crack the rest of the day—this all started in the early afternoon, and he was still going at it when I went to my cabin for a break and a nap. Anna, he was still doing it when I got up several hours later! By this point I was starving, so I ordered some food and two of the cabin crew delivered it and acted like there was nothing odd going on with the billionaire in drag smoking crack. They just put my food down and left without a word."

"How long did this go on for?"

"Oh, I don't know," she wailed. "Hours! All night! He kept on smoking, and we took turns going to our cabins for a rest. But I made sure there were always two of us in the room with him to keep the music on and play the party for him." She took a deep breath. "When I came back from my cabin Chloe and Svetlana were curled up and fast asleep, and I thought Byron was just asleep too, but when I went over to talk to him, his eyes were closed, and his skin was a funny color. When I moved his head a little to try to wake him up that's when the foamy stuff came out of his mouth. I started screaming that something was wrong, and the other girls woke up and we couldn't get him to wake up."

Her sobbing turned into hyperventilating, and I knew she was about to get hysterical again. "What are we going to do? Anna, oh my God, what are we going to do!"

These girls were my responsibility and I had to get them out of this mess clean and free, plus calm April down. "April, listen to me and do exactly as I say. Wrap the brick of coke up in a towel and go up to the deck and make sure no one is looking and throw it overboard. Leave the crack pipe and whatever's left in it on the table. Take off all his drag gear and his makeup and put it back in the trunk and then go back to your cabins. Wait a few hours until the butler is ready to set up breakfast and then you run upstairs screaming that something's wrong, and you can't wake him up. Tell Chloe and Svetlana to stay in their cabins, pretending to be asleep."

"Okay, Anna," she said, still sniffling. "I'll call you later."

We hung up, but I quickly got another call. It was Svetlana, her voice as flat and demanding. "Who's going to pay me?" she said. "The motherfucker's dead, so I can't be paid?"

I was momentarily speechless. Who asks about a payday when there's a brick of coke, a crack pipe, and the dead body of a famous billionaire in the next room?

"I'm taking his watch," she went on, her voice still cold. "I have to be paid."

"Relax," I told her quickly. "We've all been paid in advance. And you need to do exactly what April tells you."

"Oh," she said, but her voice lightened up a bit. "Well, he's dead so he won't need the watch, anyway."

"Don't you even think about it," I told her. "It's a $250,000 watch. Everyone, especially his family, knows he wears it. Do you want to spend the next five years in jail for robbing a corpse?"

There was a momentary silence, and then she said, "When can I go? I get no money sitting here now."

"Do as you wish, but if you want to be caught with a brick of coke and a dead body and try to explain that away, I'm sure the jail sentence for the brick alone is more years than your age."

She let out a heavy sigh. "Whatever," she said, and hung up.

The girls followed April's script and the captain hurried down to check on Byron. "I knew he was going to take it too far one of these nights," he said. He called for help, but Byron was long past needing any.

The obituaries all said he died from a heart attack. There was no mention of any cocaine or the harem of hot girls dressing him up in drag during his last night on earth. Money buys you a lot of things. Especially silence.

# Dungeon Dan

Every few weeks, Dan would give me a call and asked who was new, thick, and into *his thing*. He was really the only client we had that took full advantage of a dominatrix's bag of tricks. He pushed things to the edge and then he went further. Luckily, dommes usually don't offer any sexual favors and the whole operation is very much above water. Then again, how can one resist a little sensual torture, when one is in the right place at the right time.

There was this place on the Lower East Side that we booked for Dan frequently. He loved to pick out different themes for the night and he was a very creative man. His only constant was a request for women curvy and tall. We'll call the location he went to "The Box". It was a BDSM dungeon in the city catering to many, if not all, of New York City's finest freaks, subs, and dommes. Each room was decorated differently to suit various needs. The props were realistic and helped with the immersion of the scene. There was a classroom, for example, where naughty students were given corporal punishment by demanding head-masters. The wrestling room saw some of the most notorious matches between strong women and their weakling counterparts that would go on for hours until the little man was forced to surrender to the woman's power and strength. Moving to room three, the sanctum. This room was a glorious recreation of a Spanish chapel. Sinners repented to none too forgiving sisters of the cross and were forced to prove their dedication.

The pink boudoir was in room four. There, men had access to wigs, shoes, dresses, makeup, and stick-on nails so they could transform into the women they hid away inside them. Most were just innocent crossdressers, not actually in need of transition, but for some, this was the only way to live out their dreams of someone making love to them the way they needed. Down the hall, to room five, you could find the Chinese Torture Chamber, decked out in red and black with a wooden bed perfect for restraints. A ball gag helped muffle the sound of pleasure-tainted screams.

Two final rooms lay upstairs. Room six was a pristine medical examiner's office. Men would be laid on the slab and tied down while the examination was in process. Sometimes it was necessary to adjust the gurney to hold the patient upside down, for bloodletting or psychiatric evaluation. Finally, there was room seven, the largest of all the accommodations. It was a medieval holding room befitted with a breaking wheel and wooden flogs. Dommes called the breaking wheel "the wheel of fortune" for all they'd been able to get out of their subs while using it. That included money, but also confessions and immense praise.

I was not very well-acclimated with the world that domina-trices occupy. I ignorantly assumed it was all about weird, painful sex. But I was wrong. It was about humiliation, degrada-tion, and dominance, but it all points to coping and healing. I know it seems disconnected, but the essence of it all is to work through your insecurities or kinks in a place where you consent to all of them. The power dynamic is, essentially, fabricated. Powerful men *love* dommes. Escapism was also a huge selling point. However, it helps if we all just play along for our purposes here.

Dan called one morning and wanted an immediate booking. He wanted to play in both room four and then room five. "How long do you plan to stay," I asked.

"Two hours. Will she have long nails?" he panted.

"Yes, and freshly painted. She'll see you there, one p.m."

I sent Alison to The Box early, to prepare, dressed in all black with thigh-high studded boots on. The doorbell rang promptly at one and a doorman let Dan in after he showed ID. Alison was waiting for him in the pink boudoir room reading a magazine. She handed it to Dan when he walked in and told him to pick out a look. He found an image of Linda Evangelista and said, "Her. I want to look like her."

He picked out a red spandex dress and black strappy sandals. He began putting on makeup, starting with a thick layer of foundation in an attempt to cover his five o'clock shadow. Alison assisted with his blush, eyeshadow, and mink eyelash extensions. He needed help putting on his nails, getting the glue everywhere, so Alison helped with that, too. The long, pink acrylic fakes sealed the deal for Dan. "How do I look, Mistress?" Dan asked.

"You look disgusting," Alison said. "You're a vile little man. Get on your knees."

Dan fell to the floor and Alison clamped a dog collar around his throat. She made him crawl on all fours to their next destination: the Chinese Torture Chamber. She walked her pooch slowly and his stockings caught on the worn hardwood floors. She saw the rips and it was cause for punishment.

"Please, Mistress, I didn't mean to..."

"You're so clumsy and worthless. Get on the table," Alison said through gritted teeth.

"Mistress, please, I'll do anything! I'm so sorry," Dan pleaded at her feet.

"Get on the table!" she yelled, yanking Dan's collar.

Anna Gristina

Dan obeyed and climbed onto the black iron table, then laid down.

Alison dug through a drawer and let out a sinister giggle when she found what she was looking for. She took out the ball gag and fastened it around Dan's head. She restrained his arms and legs, so he was stuck face up on the table.

"I'm going to make you beg for forgiveness. Those were nice tights and you ruined them, swine," Alison sneered. She explored the closets, filled with riding crops and tasing devices. Dan emitted muffled cries through the ball gag. She cut him out of his clothing, stripping him bare. She ran her nails along his skin, gently at first but then digging into him, leaving red tracks across his arms and ribs. When she approached his thighs, she noticed he had become erect. She paused.

"You pervert. You're not allowed to be hard until I give you permission," she said, smacking his thigh with a whip. He flinched from the sting that it made. Alison started again with her nails, tickling him while he squirmed with delight. Beads of sweat had begun dripping from his forehead, past his temples, and wet the leather bands strapped around his face. She tortured him for many minutes before she relented. This was all to be expected, but Dan acted as if he hadn't been through this exact routine time after time. He ached and panted while Alison nonchalantly moved feathers and fingernails across his body, his member twitching incessantly.

"How bad do you want it, scum?" she asked. He said he needed relief like his life depended on it. She undid one of his restraints and said "You can touch yourself for thirty seconds. I'm counting now," and she did so. He went at it furiously, looking all around the room while he did so, but alas, relief did not happen in time. When his thirty seconds were up, Alison slammed a crop against his forearm. Dan begged for more time, but he would not get any for a while.

"If you want to cum so bad," she went on, "you'll have to do

130

something more to earn it." She went to the corner of the room to peer into a cabinet, producing cleaning supplies and fresh rags. "Clean this entire room, and I'll let you finish. But it has to be spotless," she explained, and pulled a white silk glove from her bag. She allowed him to get off the table, removed his ball gag, and put him to work.

Dan was in luck, because these room were cleaned after every client and never really had the chance to get very dirty, but still he took up his task as if he'd been told to do it by a drill sergeant. She reveled in his cleaning, his scrubbing on his hands and knees at the floors. As if those stockings hadn't been ruined before, they surely were now! While Dan cleaned, Alison kicked her feet up and flipped through magazines, barking out "You missed a spot!" every once in a while. It was easy money, sitting there, not even having to remove her clothes. Way easier than stripping, she reflected.

After a half hour, Dan reported that he had finished cleaning and wished for his mistress to inspect his work. He had sweated nearly all his makeup off, and the straps of his dress were continually falling down as he stood against the wall while Alison ran two fingers over every surface, inspecting the glove all the while. She found not a speck of dust.

"What a good job you did, worm. You have three minutes to get hard and finish before I send you away. You may begin," she said, straight-faced. Dan began right away, and it only took him two minutes to get there. He finished, groaning loudly and breathlessly. Then, he promptly left the room without a word, not even a "thank you". That was how it always was with him. He waltzed out of there like nothing had happened, but I could tell, every time he called, that he was always thinking about his next fix.

# Half-Off

L ike any other business, Monday mornings brought about an influx of clients calling after a weekend of having the phone lines unopen. The men who used my service had strict schedules, with every hour accounted for the days, weeks, and months ahead. Over the weekend, they often penciled in time with one of my girls and when Monday rolled around, they were quick to call in order to arrange next weekend's appointment. It was almost like their own form of therapy, I imagine, a time to escape from the powerhouse meetings and high-stakes negotiations. On a more practical note, they also needed to call to receive that week's updated password for the company's client website, where they could view new faces and get an idea for who they might be interested in. So, yes, Mondays were busy as soon as I opened the phone lines.

There was a lot of predictability in those calls, but a lot of uncertainty, too. We heard from new clients all the time who usually got our number from the classified ads, or perhaps a friend passed it along. After the initial Monday mania, sometime in the afternoon, I got a call from a new gent, a voice I did not recognize but sounded pleasant over the phone. He was an older guy, he explained, and he was very well-spoken. I thought maybe he was a retired lawyer or something of that nature from the way he conducted himself so professionally. He was very careful to keep his words nonincriminating which, thank goodness, was what we requested of anyone who called in. It was crucial that clients understood our code of conduct, as it were. For example, asking if full service was included was a huge red flag that someone had no idea what they were doing or how to conduct themselves with a business like mine. I hung up immediately when I heard questions like that, without hesitation. It was something that happened regularly and I'm sure I lost hundreds of high-paying clients because of it, but one can never be too careful when the risk is lifetimes in prison and, much more importantly, the loss of seeing one's children every day. I couldn't avoid it entirely, but I did my best for my kids. I recall a friend telling me that "greed gets you every time" and I took that to heart. Even if girls were begging me for work or I was tight on funds, a loud-mouth rich kid would always get a dial tone from me.

Fortunately, such was not the case with the well-spoken gentleman on the phone that day. He mentioned that he had seen the ad for a "former centerfold model seeking affluent gentleman for a mutually rewarding relationship" that had been placed in the *New York Observer*. I always had great luck with the men who saw ads placed in that paper, probably because it was smaller and mostly subscribed to by the wealthy, though it was available at a few newspaper stands around the city. The calls were few and far between, but they were always from well-off, well-educated men, the sort that was also brought in by the *International Herald Tribune*. It's too bad neither is in print anymore; I'm sure someone holding my former position could get great use out of their readership the way I used to.

Our conversation was a great example of how I wish every call with a new client went. He expressed his interest after seeing the ad and I told him about Lisa, the former Playboy model in her thirties who was looking for one or two exclusive gentlemen for an ongoing arrangement. I made him aware of her rate; $1,000 an hour with a two-hour minimum, outcall only. He said his name was Hank and I thanked him for calling us, putting on my best flirty customer service voice while I went through the screening process with him. As with most new callers, the screening went unnoticed and was thought of as polite conversation. For me, it was both.

"Hank," I said, "we are a very small, shall I say, unnoticed, private club that is incredibly exclusive when it comes to choosing members. It is important to us that we keep a low profile. May I ask, what is your line of work?"

"That all sounds perfect to me. I'm retired now, but I used to practice real estate law and I'd done so since receiving my degree after completing my time in the military," Hank said.

"Well, thank you for your service! I'm glad you mentioned it because veterans receive a ten percent discount."

"That's very kind, I appreciate that. Though you might need to tack it back on. I hope it's not a problem, but I do have a disability due to an injury I sustained during combat."

"It's not a problem at all. I'll let Lisa know, but I'm sure she won't think anything of it. So, you said seven p.m. at the Carlyle Lounge and Bar, this weekend?"

"Yes, that'd be great. But please don't forget to tell her about my disability. I don't want her to be uncomfortable" he said, sounding nervous.

"I'll let Lisa know. Thank you, Hank."

After I hung up with Hank, I gave Lisa a call to let her know about the booking.

I told her that he sounded incredibly sweet on the phone, and she was excited to meet him. I mentioned what he wished me to, and Lisa was eager to accept; she had no qualms or reservations just as I thought. Her only question was about what she should wear because, if I'm recalling correctly, it was her first time going to the Carlyle. I reminded her that the hotel has a rather upscale and modest dress code, so she shouldn't wear anything too flashy or attention-grabbing. Other than that, the only thing left to do was to text Hank about the confirmation and let him know about sending us his room number after his check-in.

The rest of the day came and went, as usual, with weekly regulars checking in about a new interest they had and seeing if additional photos were available. We'd send some by email if there were some on hand. Over the years, we got to know regulars so well I could tell if the girl he liked would be a good fit for him. Matchmaking was a huge part of the service I provided, so I paid close attention to how dates went and saw to it that each client was followed up with so he could rate his experience with the girl he booked. That attention to detail was a major component of our longstanding success.

The day of Lisa and Hank's date came around and Lisa called in right on time at 6:55 as she walked into the Hotel's lounge area. She sat herself at the bar and ordered a martini to sip while she waited for Hank to come down. Within a few minutes, she spotted an older man with a limp heading toward the bar. She smiled and waved at him, standing to greet him. He walked with a cane but moved at a fine pace, especially for a man his age.

"Your photos don't do you justice," Hank said. "You're much more beautiful in person." Lisa blushed and thanked him. They made a great first impression on each other and spent the next thirty minutes chatting and getting to know each other over a couple of cocktails. I got a text saying "we've met and everything's going great" from Lisa, which was always good to hear. I responded by reminding her to let me know when she leaves or if she plans to stay the night and went back to updating the private members' site.

They went up to his room together, where Hank opened a nice bottle of wine to go with the light appetizers he'd ordered from room service. They continued to talk, warming up to each other all the while, until Hank asked if it would be okay for them to get more comfortable. Lisa nodded demurely so Hank excused himself to freshen up in the bathroom. She thought about how nice he was being while she removed her dress and revealed her favorite La Perla underwear set. She could hear the water running in the bathroom, then a heavy clunk. Hank grunted as he opened the door, using his hands to walk across the room, while his legs cut off above the knee dragged soundlessly across the floor. With surprising ease, he hoisted himself onto the couch beside Lisa. Now, there was no issue at all, but she was a bit taken aback by this development. She knew he had a disability, but she didn't expect him to be a double amputee when he had been walking so well earlier.

"Please don't be scared," he started. "I lost my legs during the war, but I've got pretty strong arms for a man my age." He looked a bit uncomfortable as he waited for her response, worried she might react as other women had in his past.

Lisa took a deep breath and swallowed her initial shock. "It doesn't bother me a bit, honey. You've still got the leg that matters, don't you?" she said playfully, putting her hand near his hip. He liked that, it made him feel good that she was being playful with him about it, and he moved off the sofa at an alarmingly quick rate and went to the bed, using the side table to help himself up. Sure, it was a new experience for Lisa, being with a man who had no legs, but he was such a darling and the rest of their time together went off without a hitch.

When they finished up their fun, Hank went back into the bathroom and came out a few minutes later walking a bit taller, and not just because of his prosthetics. He paid Lisa her fee and a sizable tip. He did make a joke that he should maybe only be charged half of what a regular john would pay because he was only "half the man". It was a good one, I had to admit, and he went on to make that same joke about getting a half-off special with dozens of ladies he booked through us during his time as a regular.

# Voyeuristic Ventures

Most of my clients liked to keep their activities behind closed doors. Surely, they weren't shy when it came to having models around on their yachts or attending their private parties, but overall, their indulgences happened in private. You never know who might be watching and so much of what they were paying for was discretion. Secrecy worked for me and my girls, anyway. It helped everyone feel more comfortable to be as they were in the seclusion of hotel rooms and private residences.

That practice didn't work for everyone, though. For some, the more public, the better. Voyeurism wasn't hugely popular with my clients, but I definitely had a couple who were into it. It did make things complicated and, I'll admit, a tad nerve-wracking. I'll begin by telling you more about someone you've already met.

Mr. Strange. Yes, he was such an oddball he made it in twice. I did mention he had a thing for public stunts on London Bridge and I thought I might elaborate on that.

This request was mostly made while he was still living in London and booking through Vera. However, once he'd lived in the States for a while, he booked through me even when he traveled back home to England for extended stays. On those occasions, I got to better understand what Vera meant when she said she had a gentleman proclaiming, "London Bridge is cumming now".

Before my time with him, he stuck to a predictable script, with the girl being the only variable. Then again, Mr. Strange was a mostly predictable guy when it came to his every day, regular life. He donned a white or light blue, heavily starched shirt beneath a pinstripe suit. When he was in London, he wore a long London fog coat overtop to combat the constant rain. He was completely unassuming, from his charming good looks to his status as a major shareholder in a large hedge fund. He was also the CEO of his company, but he was a soft-spoken person, generally. That coat he wore was like a key into the adventurous world of sex acts on London Bridge, and those acts were like his gateway drug.

Normally, after his workday came to a close, he'd walk with the same herd of associates to the bus stop. A few times a month, he'd diverge from the pack as silently as possible and walk to the center of London Bridge, carrying a copy of *The Times* and a bouquet of white carnations. He could also be recognized by the work ID clipped to his coat and the frantic way he looked from side to side, swaying slightly as he did so. The woman of the hour would approach him a few minutes after he arrived after making sure no one was paying attention to him while he stood there.

"Are you Albert?" she asked.

"Yes," he responded, breathing heavily.

"I'm going to do things to you, and I don't want to hear any arguments," she whispered, slipping a fake gun from her bag and pressing the muzzle against his side.

"What do you want from me? Don't hurt me!"

"I won't if you do what I say. Take your cock out and touch it slowly."

"Are you mad? We're in public."

"Do it or I drop you right here," she dug the gun deeper into his side, but to passersby, it simply looked like a couple huddling together, gazing across the water. Mr. Strange used his right hand to pull the middle of his coat forward, fashioning it as a barrier between his manhood and the eyes of others. The woman shielded him from the left side, and he pulled out his member, already sporting a semi. He stroked himself to life while the woman watched, making threats as he got harder and harder. When he was as big as he could get, she'd take notice of how well-endowed he was and make a flattering remark, keeping him interested with her genuine amazement. He was usually sweating by then, either from the excitement or from the fact that he wore that overcoat even in warmer months so he could partake in this activity.

"I want you to masturbate while you tell me all the dirty things you want to do to me," she'd say, pulling her own jacket slightly to the side to reveal that she wasn't wearing any panties. This was risky business, a huge factor in why it was difficult to find girls who would participate, but it made Mr. Strange nearly burst with lust.

"I'd bend you over the railing and slam my cock deep inside you, fucking you 'til you were begging me to stop. I'd make you wait to cum 'til I was done with you," he said, moving his hand faster and faster, gripping himself tightly. People who were passing behind him might've heard his labored breathing, might've even seen his left upper arm moving rapidly against the woman who stood beside him, but they said nothing. Feeling their curious or judgmental eyes across his back was like being walked in on at the gym showers, wondering what they saw and what they thought when they saw it.

She noticed he was getting close to finishing, so she got up close to his ear and whispered, "I bet you would baby. I'd want you to lift me up on that railing and fuck me raw. I'd cum so loud the Queen could hear it through the walls of Buckingham fucking Palace."

With that, he could bear it no longer. He released his seed, leaning forward so it wouldn't get on his nicely pressed slacks. He pulled an initialed hanky from his pocket, wiped his hands, and pulled his coat tightly around him. From an interior pocket, he'd hand over an envelope thick with cash, then he walked off amongst the crowd that unwittingly played a part in his fantasy.

The next gent with similar interests had slightly more decency than Mr. Strange. He only subjected one person to his voyeurism in any direct way, while others were just left confused or concerned without offense. Every week, without fail, Ken would call to schedule his weekend kidnapping. I don't even know how he found the time for something like this, seeing that Ken ran one of the best-known Wall Street firms and was constantly inundated with board meetings and phone calls. I guess it goes to show that people make time for what's important to them.

He called on Mondays and the gig would go down on Thursdays at 4:30 p.m. He would specifically ask for women who were athletic and open-minded. I kept a running list of qualified candidates since he didn't like to see the same women more than a few times. It was a constant effort to network and grow my roster to keep up with his consistent desire for new faces. When I did present him with someone new, he'd ask questions like *"How tall is she?"* or *"Could she wrestle me, do you think?"* if that gives you any hint of what he was looking for. I'd book his Thursday appointment with two girls, one new and one who he'd been with before a time or two. It made for a smooth operation.

Being so neurotic about his schedule, he'd call again each Wednesday to confirm that everything was in place. He'd double-check on the capabilities of each girl and ask if I was sure they'd be into it. I promised that I had found him the perfect pair, each of them strong as an ox and over six feet tall. I also told him what they planned to wear so he knew who to watch out for. I advised the girls beforehand to make sure they wore running shoes because they'd be needing them.

Each week brought about a slightly different theme to initiate the new face, but overall, it was the same each week. At four o'clock, outside the Plaza Hotel, my two ladies would be waiting for a limo to pick them up. The backseat of the limo had already been filled with bondage gear and adult toys, including strap-ons and small flogs. There was also a map that the ladies would be needing for their mission. They settled in and the driver took the pair to a park entrance. From there, they could spot Ken jogging around in shorts so little they were riding up his ass crack and a tight, white t-shirt. He looked like an 80s gym teacher and the girls chuckled when they saw him, but soon regained their demeanor. They had a serious task ahead of them after all, pulling off the kidnapping of a Wall Street millionaire.

The driver, upon arriving, rolled up the partition, the ladies signal to get the party started. One of the girls rolled down the window, calling Ken over to show him the map and ask him for directions. While he looked it over, she opened the door and both the girls attempted to pull him into the car. He attempted to run away, but they took off after him, catching him only a few feet from the parked car. They dragged him towards it kicking and screaming. God only knows why a fleet of cop cars were never summoned by a passerby witnessing this crazy scene. I'm sure it looked legitimately concerning, but New Yorkers are known for minding their business, which certainly worked in Ken's favor. He was thrown into the backseat and the limo driver took off, following instructions given prior to circle the park and stay off busy streets.

Ken was tied up and ball-gagged while the girls had their way with him. They called him a horrible man and told him he deserved all the punishment he was getting. It took about an hour from start to finish, with the kidnapping coming to end with Ken being pushed out of the car, concealed bottom red and welted, and the girls threatening to come for him again if he was bad. Then the driver would drop the girls off where he had picked them up, handing each her payment for the completion of another successful assignment.

# Ladies on the Rocks

T he day began like any other. I woke up, fed the pets, and walked the dogs while my kids finished breakfast and got ready for school. When the last of my four children was on the bus, I took a deep breath. Watching them every day go off to learn and grow, completely unaware of what their mum's job was, gave my heart a bit of a twist. I wanted to protect them of course, but I wanted to provide for them first. They were at the core of everything I strove to do in my life. When I got back inside, I decided to open the phone line a little earlier than usual. It must've been a bit of intuition because it started ringing right away, even though my regulars knew my hours like the back of their hands. I hesitated to pick up, worried I might be setting a new precedent that would quickly get around. Money is money though, so I answered. A posh sounding Englishman was on the other end inquiring about an ad we had placed for a lovely woman named Grace. This was the typical way a conversation began with a promising newcomer. We went through the motions, and I gave him my name, so things felt personal and comfortable. He told me his name was Thomas.

Grace, the girl from the ad, was of average height and was

studying at the Fashion Institute of Technology in the city, making her schedule fairly limited. Thomas asked if her skin was as fair in person as it appeared in her pictures, and I assured him that it was. I noticed, from the caller ID, that he was calling from the Four Seasons, which didn't trip any alarms in my head. Most undercover cop calls came in from cheap hotels, while the Four Seasons' rooms were $600 or more.

I relayed all the information I had on Grace to Thomas's excited approval. He sounded like an easygoing gentleman, even letting me in on how his trip to New York was going and what he was in town for. Through relaxed chitchat, I assessed if Thomas was legit or not. I didn't notice anything strange, except for the fact that he was looking for someone who was ready to take on a challenge. For regulars, that was a fine thing to say. For new clients, however, it caused a smidge of unease. Not enough for me not to book him, granted, but a little bit. There were no other red flags, so no reason not to try him out. I called around and gauged other girls' interest in case Grace wasn't up for adventure. When I did eventually call her, I let her know that he sounded perfectly pleasant on the phone and if she did have any availability for a mystery client, I thought she'd have a good time because he was definitely interested in her. To my relief, she agreed! I made arrangements for them to meet at 7:45 p.m. in the hotel lobby, on the 57th Street side. He requested she wear blue eyeliner and dress for dinner.

When Grace arrived, she was greeted by a charming man in his early fifties. Thomas was in great shape, not just for his age but in general, and his salt and pepper hair only added to his charm. He held his arm out to Grace and escorted her to their reservation at The Garden, the hotel's restaurant. The food and atmosphere were enamoring, and Grace found herself quite enthralled with our handsome new man. Over dessert, he complimented her looks, but also her wit and style. She told him all about the courses she was taking and her dreams of Fashion

Week and runways. She didn't want the spotlight, she explained, rather she wanted the culture. He listened intently until their plates were cleared and the time had come to move things to the bedroom. Before they took off, though, Thomas wanted to give Grace some insight.

"I'm a simple man, Grace," Thomas said. "I'd never dream of disrespecting any woman. My parents raised me to treat every lady as kind as if she were my own mother. But I have a quirk, one I cannot begin to understand. I'm hoping you can help me with it tonight."

"It would be my pleasure," Grace said, urging him to go on.

"I've got the tub up in my room filled with ice water," he said with lowered voice, "and so I want to put some blue lipstick on you and have you lay in the bath until your body temperature is slightly lower. Then, I'll lift you, but you have to stay completely still. I'll bring you to the bed and then I'll...well, you get the picture. I'll pay you anything you deem reasonable."

Grace contemplated his request. It was like nothing she'd been asked to do before. She wondered how extensively this fetish permeated Thomas's mind and for how long. All his life? Was it a recent development? A blank check had to be seriously considered, no matter the request. Grace thought for a moment about what she should ask for, settling on an additional $1,500 atop the regular fee. She probably could've asked for much more, but she wasn't trying to swindle the man; she simply chose her fee according to what she thought was fair. Before she went upstairs with him, she gave me a quick call to make sure her decision was okay. Of course, it was, and the additional fee she negotiated would be hers alone. I was a businesswoman managing other businesswomen, so what they achieved out there on their own was not mine to take.

They reached the room and went straight to the bathroom. Just as Thomas had said, the tub was filled with ice water. One could feel the coolness of it if they held their hand above the surface. On the counter, Grace saw the light blue lipstick, which she picked up and put on after using a tissue to remove her pink gloss. When it was on, it made her pale skin look all the more pallid, but she had to admit it looked sort of cool. Like Halloween makeup. Thomas waited on the bed while she disrobed and slid into the frigid water, so cold it stung.

"I'm in the water," she shouted to Thomas, already shivering.

"Good! I'll be in to get you soon!"

After about eight minutes, Grace was tempted to bail. It seemed as if she'd been waiting forever, and her shivering had given way to numbness. Just as she was ready to give up, Thomas entered, so she closed her eyes and tried to control her breathing. He easily lifted her lithe but limp body from the bath and carried her to the bed, placing her down gently. The room's AC was blasting, keeping it as cool as a morgue. Grace's chest rose and fell undetectably, which pleased Thomas greatly. He took a towel from the bathroom and dried Grace off a little, careful not to leave the towel on her too long for fear she'd warm up. He watched her as he unbuttoned his trousers and shirt, moving his garments to a chair. He moved onto the bed next to her and caressed her cold legs with his fingertips, giving her goosebumps and making her shiver. He ran his fingers all over her body, over her erect nipples and taut stomach. He smelled her hair. His breath sped up when he gazed at this lifeless beauty, making his member harden.

He positioned himself on top of her, placing his penis between her freezing thighs, then humping her slowly. Internally, Grace was relishing in the warmth his body was passing into hers, never mind the sex. She'd let him lay on her all day if it meant finally getting thawed out. After a few moments, she felt a warm wetness between her thighs, and Thomas rolled off her. He went into the bathroom again, retrieving a towel to wipe up the little mess he made on his corpse mistress, as well as a toasty robe to revive her with. That was all that was required, and he thanked her explicitly for her participation.

"You probably think I'm a monster, wanting to do something like that," he admitted, rubbing his hands over his face. They were just sitting in the bed together, Grace pulling the covers ever tighter around her.

"Why would I think that?"

"It's disgusting. I don't know how I've ended up like this."

"I don't know, either. I don't think there's anything wrong with you. But you've never..."

"Oh, God, of course not. I've wondered, though, if it would be the same. I have a feeling it wouldn't be. I have no intention of finding out." Grace put her hand out for him to hold. The shame he felt wasn't completely relieved, but it helped that he had talked to her about it. It made him feel not so alone in the world. "Thank you, for all this. You were perfect," he said and smiled at her.

Thomas became a regular and a favorite among the girls for his generosity and kindness. For over fifteen years, he never changed his script, nor did he ever get stingy with what he was willing to pay. No one could refuse that kind of client, even if we couldn't fully understand the man beneath the kink. Sometimes, you just have to accept that the world is a confusing and unclear place, a place where we are not meant to understand all that is presented to us.

# Girls Night

E very so often the girls and I would arrange for a night out to blow off steam and unleash all the gossip we'd kept pent up. There weren't many opportunities one had to discuss their job in our industry, and many of the stories collected here in these pages were topics of conversation during our girls' nights. There are hundreds more that didn't make it this book! We could talk for hours and hours about the gentleman they were seeing, the oddities they'd run into, and the way their jobs were helping them make progress in their various personal lives. To their families, the girls were flight stewardesses, beauticians, or realtors. We all had cover stories to protect our livelihoods. We really couldn't go to our loved ones with all the craziness and stress of our lives, so we were so lucky to have each other.

I closed up the phone lines early on Fridays, so we didn't get inundated with calls from lonely divorcés, angry singles, and party animals looking for some quick tail. The weekends were for scheduled dates and a bit of relaxation after a hard week's work. When it worked out that a bunch of the ladies were off one Friday night, I planned a little dinner and dancing.

Our first stop of the evening was a great Indian buffet spot.

We had our fill of kebabs, spicy soups, and samosas before piling into two cabs, bringing us to Culture Club, an 80s themed dance club. We boogied till our feet hurt and had an amazing time letting our hair down. All of us, we were about seven that night, headed back to one of the girl's apartments. Now, some of the girls indulged in this more often than myself, but we all deserved it, so we lit and drank a few fruity cocktails, reveling in each other's company. It was the perfect night to just chill out. This was our version of watercooler talk and it felt good to get out the stories we'd be holding in. We'd go around the room talking about who had the oddest caller lately, which is how I heard about so many of the crazy men I've been telling you about! It was no different than any other girls' night, just shooting the breeze about whose sugar daddy had the biggest apartment and where the best surgeons could be found. Admittedly, I suppose the topics could be a little different than what other ladies discussed with their friends, but the heart of it was all the same. It made us feel close when, at times, our industry could feel isolating. There happened to be this one girl there, Rachael, who had a story unlike any of the other girls, and she was kind enough to open up to us that night in a very intimate way.

Rachael came to me through a referral from a longtime industry friend, Christy. Christy had known Rachael for years and told me that because she was so beautiful, men just fell at her feet. We scheduled a meeting at a small restaurant I frequented on the Upper East Side. I awaited her arrival at my table by the window. When I saw from the window a stunning brunette strutting down the sidewalk, I nearly fell out of my chair. She walked in, nearly six feet tall with a Jessica Rabbit body and double her sex appeal. It was clear why men were so obsessed; I don't know if I ever met a woman as gorgeous as her, to this very day.

She asked for Anna's table when she walked in, greeting me

with a smile and an elegant handshake. We ordered some cock-tails and something light to eat.

"I'm so glad we were able to meet today. Christy had nothing but good things to say about you," I said, already subconsciously endearing myself to her. Normally, it seems like it would be the other way around, girls trying to make a good impression, but her good looks were almost intimidating, even to me.

"Christy's too good. I couldn't wait to meet with you after she made the suggestion. I've really been wanting to get into this line of work." Her voice was sultry even in this business setting. It had a somewhat raspy, "just-waking-up" quality to it.

"So I've heard. I wanted to ask why that might be? It's not as easy as you might think."

"I'm prepared for whatever it takes. I've been through a lot as a woman, and I know that being around others who have chosen this path will help me feel like, a sense a community. Not to mention the financial freedom that I'm hoping to gain." She seemed confident in her answer and continued to be sure of herself as we spoke. Even early in the interview, she was showing signs of being a promising addition to the roster.

I asked her to tell me more about herself, about her life. She said she was thirty-two (she didn't look a day over twenty-four) and had gone to college at a state university in New Jersey. I checked her various forms of ID to make sure she was of age, since one can never be too careful, and we hit it off like old schoolmates. There was no denying her flawless nature. She had grace, was super personable, and the kind of woman that the rest of us shot daggers at out of sheer envy. I asked if she'd be avail-able anytime soon for a photo shoot, so we could get her pictures circulating in ads and on our website. She eagerly said she was available immediately. We had a pleasant lunch and parted ways, but I arranged her shoot as soon as I got home. At the time, I was using a photographer named Benny who'd been shooting my girls for about a year and a half. He did great work, and always made the girls look natural and comfortable even when they weren't the best models. A pretty face does not a model make, mind you. I knew Rachael's pictures would come out pretty, but what I got was beyond expectations. It was the most amazing camera work I'd ever seen. She was a complete natural in front of the camera and extremely photogenic. Her pictures belonged on the cover of *Playboy*, no doubt about it. Delighted by the photos, I asked when she was free over the next week. Again, she said she was available whenever I needed her; she was ready to work, needed the money, and was eager to meet someone. She had also taken some personal photos, on her dime, and wanted to show them to me. I agreed, and it would not be the last time I saw a whole lot of Rachael.

Her first few bookings went great, each one going over the two-hour minimum and leaving her with generous tips. By then, I realized what a rare find I had encountered. She was worthy of A-level status, which had me on the phones personally calling some of the bigger fish I knew, upping her introduction fee and limiting her availability.

I was able to book her all summer long, even when things were slow otherwise. The other girls were a little jealous, but Rachael was just really popular. There wasn't much I could do to slow her down. She had completely open availability and loved going out with our high caliber clients. She was still looking for a consistent sugar daddy and, if she found him, things would open back up for my other ladies. I hoped she would find him quickly, so I didn't have a mutiny on my hands.

Finally, a super handsome, sweet engineer from the West Coast took a shine to her and was considering the idea of her moving to LA and being his girl. She was excited, but since it wasn't set up and agreed to yet, she continued to go on dates, her sugar daddy hopes remaining on-hold.

One such date unraveled it all. One night, an old, Argentinian friend called. He was a successful billionaire in a worldwide mineral mining operation. He wanted to meet Rachael after viewing her photos on the site. They agreed to meet for a light dinner around 8:30 p.m., then some cocktails. They'd see what happened from there. If there were a connection, she might spend the night and go with him to Atlantic City. She called around 11:00 pm, and said all was well, that she would like to stay over and make the trip to AC. They planned on leaving around 5:00 a.m. the next day. She would call me when she arrived. I was overjoyed by this news since making money in any industry has its highs and lows and things had been extremely quiet until Rachael came along.

Around 1:00 am, I received a call, which was very out of the ordinary, but if I had a lady out on a date, I always slept with the phone on loud next to my bed. It was Rachael saying that she was leaving. I asked her what had changed her mind. She said her date was tired and decided to go to Atlantic City another time, so she was going home in a cab. I asked her to call me when she got home, so I knew she was safe.

Moments later, I received a call from the gent screaming at me through the phone in his heavy Argentinian accent. It turned out our Rachael had a secret, and he was pissed about it. I had to refund him for the time he had spent with her so he would continue booking other girls with us. He was too lucrative a client to lose, unfortunately. I called Rachael back.

"Is it true?" I asked. I could hear road noise, distant car horns, but otherwise Rachael was silent. "I need to know."

Finally, she spoke, but very quietly. "Yes."

"Why didn't you tell me earlier? This could've been incredibly dangerous, for you and for me!"

"I can't talk about it now and I'm exhausted. Can't it wait until the morning?" She sounded like she was beginning to cry. We left it there. That was the last date I was able to send her on, sadly, but she came around for a while after, and told us what all she had been through before joining our ranks during that evening of gossip and truth-sharing. That was when everyone, myself included, got the full story.

She'd had a long-term boyfriend for two years before she got gender confirmation surgery. It was the last piece to the puzzle she'd been trying to solve since she was a child. All her life, she'd been spiritually feminine, but outwardly she was a confused kid. When she got older, she was able to finally transition and live her life as the woman she always knew she would become.

"One day," she told us as we gathered around her, "we got into a huge fight. I stormed out and went to my mom's to cool down for a couple days. He was being a real asshole when it came to the recovery time of the surgery. I was almost there, but I still needed a few weeks before we could be intimate again. It wasn't even my choice; those were doctor's orders! And even if it had been technically long enough, I was allowed to take as long as I wanted. Anyway, I eventually went back to our apartment, maybe a week or so later, and I smelled something awful. I…I went into our bathroom, and he was…" she stopped. Her voice had caught, and she started to cry, tears falling from her olive cheeks. She could hardly get the words out when she told us how she had walked in on her boyfriend, dead on the bathroom floor, with half his face eaten off by the two starving dogs they shared. He had overdosed, but she didn't know it had been an accident or not. After that, she didn't want to fall in love again. That's why she had sought out work in escort. Now, I realized, I had become another person who rejected her and hurt her because of who she was, because I had let her go after we found out.

The predicament was much more complicated than meets the eye. I didn't fire her because she was transgender. I fired her because I couldn't change her status on the site after she'd been out with so many guys who weren't aware she had transitioned. If they found out, and felt tricked, they could leave, and I could lose my business being that she'd been with some of the highest paying gents I had. I couldn't send her out while keeping her transition a secret, because if someone suspected, it could be incredibly dangerous for her. I was utterly stuck between a rock and a hard place. There was just no way to go about keeping her without a significant risk one way or another, so in the end, I had to break the bad news to her.

It was more evidence of her good heart that there weren't any hard feelings. That's why I was still happy to invite her to the girls' nights. After she had told us about her past, tons of hugs and kisses were exchanged which helped brighten everyone's spirits again. We got back to lighthearted chatter and some of the girls got curious about Rachael's other experiences, like if sex was different for her or if she still even liked it after surgery.

Let's get one thing straight, Rachael was far from shy. Those personal pictures she had shown me when I first hired her had been completely nude shots, full spread eagle! That was why I never could've suspected, everything about her was one hundred percent woman! The other girls, I suppose, were still having trouble believing she hadn't been born female and she was intent on proving some things to us.

"Let me show you what a $25,000 pussy looks like, ladies," Rachael said, standing up. We all were hooting and hollering, cross-faded and acting like crazy college girls. "Now, I may not have been born with a vagina, but I *was* born a girl, and I paid good money to make that known to everyone who sees me and fucks me, too." Rachael went to the large ottoman in the middle of the room, laid on her back, and hiked up her mini skirt. She pulled aside a dental floss-thin thong and there before us, between a set of stunningly long tan legs, was probably the most picture-perfect genitalia any of us had ever seen. I tried to stand back, in an attempt to be reserved and professional, but I peeked from behind the other girls and was quite stunned. The peanut gallery was letting loose a chorus of *oohs* and *ahhs*, while one of the girls exclaimed "it's better than mine!" I think that was the overall sentiment because after that I heard there was a pretty big uptick in vaginal rejuvenation procedures in the city. Well, if you're a plastic surgeon looking for someone to thank for that trend, I can direct you to Rachael. It was a night I won't soon forget. Some of the best laughs and therapy sessions were had in those sweet little gatherings of ladies who trusted each other with the secrets of life as a working woman.

# Piano Man Seeks Cinderella

Not every gent was willing to pull out all the stops for a night with one of my girls, but James was the exception. He was a romantic older gentleman who would slick back his salt and pepper hair, style his mustache, and show up as if he were on his way to the Met Gala. Considering his entanglement with old Hollywood glamour, he'd have his dates prepare by sending them on a hunt for lingerie, a formal gown, and give them a spa day, all on his dime. He simply had a flair for opulence.

With that being said, James was a huge hit with the ladies he booked, and he booked regularly, lucky for them. It was fun for them, getting all dressed up in elegant dresses and fancy hair styles. The only pain was the head-to-toe waxing he required before hand, but most of them were getting that done anyhow. They'd chatter back and forth about how good he smelled and how well he tipped; I couldn't get them to stop fawning over him! His dates were infamous for their luxury and intimacy.

The date began with a limo picking up his chosen lady at her place. She was brought to a private piano bar, with the driver walking her to the door and opening it for her. The entire night, she'd be treated like a queen.

She walked to the coat check, giving them her fur shawl, then wandered through an arched doorway. There, she was met by a man dressed in a fine suit.

"Your name, ma'am?"

"Beth Leaman," she responded.

"Ms. Leaman, how pleased we are that you've arrived. Allow me to escort you to your booth," he said, holding out his hand. They walked through double doors into a beautifully dim room with gentle yellow lights illuminating each table while still keeping an air of total privacy. There were vibrant indoor plants and, there in the corner upon a low, wide platform, stood a grand piano - like none other she'd ever seen - with a delicate trellis design etched into its rosewood body. The pianist played like the two were bonded from birth.

Beth was seated in the booth closest to the piano and she watched the man play until the waiter came and took her drink order, relaying that "Mr. Reynolds would be arriving shortly." He returned with her glass of red wine, as well as a three-tiered platter of small appetizers. He carefully explained what each one was and what she could expect from the experience of enjoying them, then he gave a small bow and left her again. The room around her was extraordinary. The floor-to-ceiling windows were of obscured glass, so the atmosphere was simultaneously open but cozy. It was clear that they cared not about fitting as many tables as possible because there was plenty of space even as more couples sat down.

Sipping her wine, Beth tried a few of the samplings while she watched the pianist finish and stand for gentle but enthusiastic applause. He just melted the crowd. About five minutes later, who other than the pianist himself approached Beth's table and held out his hand to her. The mysterious Mr. James Reynolds had finally arrived for his date. Beth stood to introduce herself and he spun her around, looking her up and down with voracious eyes. He muttered but two words in response to her beauty: "flawless creature." Beth blushed as she realized the whole place was looking at them, still enthralled with James's playing and most likely wishing there was more in store.

"Your playing was phenomenal, Mr. Reynolds," Beth said in the midst of their small talk.

"Oh, please, call me James. It's my name outside of this place." He went on to tell her about how he'd been playing since he was four years old and had toured the world for many years as a young man. The piano was his passion and his occupation, a fortunate combination that not many other artists can claim. The waiter came back with an exquisite bottle of wine and poured a little into a glass, allowing James to taste it before pouring more. A few other patrons stopped by the table to compliment James on his playing, to which he nodded and thanked them graciously. Beth was finding herself more and more comfortable as the date when on, almost like it was a regular date rather than a date with a john. James was so handsome and easy to talk to, even though he looked the part of a movie star and was being treated as such. When the dessert trolley came around, James had Beth pick something out for them to share. It was as amazing as everything else had been, a delectable chocolate mousse cake topped with pomegranate compote. As the waiter placed the dessert and coffees on the table, James asked that he have their coats ready to go. They finished quickly and James placed Beth's wrap around her shoulders. They walked out without ever seeing a bill, making the night that much more a celebrity experience.

They walked down the sidewalk arm in arm until they reached an old brownstone just a few blocks from the piano bar. Statues stood guard at the door. The interior was warm and professionally decorated. Through the foyer and into a large living room, James led Beth with a charming smile on his face. She was swooning over this man! When she was able to pull her gaze from him, she saw, there in the middle of the room, another magnificent grand piano up on a two-step stage, with bright lights spotlighting it.

"Gorgeous, why don't you take a look in the other room, just through that door over there. Pick out a new dress and put on some red lipstick for me, won't you?" Beth realized now the interesting part of the night was about to begin. She opened the door and found it was essentially a large walk-in closet, filled with dresses and wigs styled in 1940s fashion. Beth wandered around the room for a bit, touching the fabric and what seemed to her to be real human hairpieces. She carefully selected a tea-length fitted gown with a sweetheart neckline. It was easy to slip on, which she thought would come in handy. She also pinned up her dark hair and put on a blonde, shoulder-length wig. In the mirror, she inspected her petite figure and thought she looked just like Rita Hayworth.

James was sitting on the piano bench when she made her entrance. As she moved across the floor, coming around to the side of the stage, she noticed he was naked from the waist down. He motioned for her to sit beside him. He put her hands atop his and started to play, singing to her as he did so. He had an alluring voice from what I've heard; he was a man of many talents. The song came to a conclusion just as James's erection grew to full attention.

"I think I'm ready for more dessert. Does that sound good, my love?"

Beth nodded eagerly, so James lifted her and plopped her on the piano's lid. He pulled her dress up around her waist and took her panties off. He began to tease her pearl, his mustache tickling her. By now, Beth was desperate to have him, which is very uncommon in my industry. James was just one of those guys that a girl could fall in love with. He licked her like a dripping ice cream cone in the summer, then she heard the unmistakable crinkle of plastic. He entered her with fervor, and they finished together, her crying out with pleasure.

Out of all the men, and especially out of all the lovers, James was the only one women wanted to see multiple times. Something about musicians, I think. They really know what they're doing with their fingers.

# Dr. Roadkill

In the days of operating the in-call house, one of our weekly clients was the city's top pediatric neurosurgeon. His booked slot was Thursdays around one or two p.m. I'd see Gerald on the security camera, wearing his brown corduroy slacks and tweed checkered jacket over a blue shirt, the top button always left undone. His tie was never quite done up correctly, like no one had ever taught him how to do it. Under his arm, he carried the *New York Times* and an old leather portfolio. He'd give me a speedy "hello" before bolting into the first room on the right of the hall. I'd send the girls in that were on staff for the evening, but only if they had size seven to seven and a half feet. As they walked through and introduced themselves, he'd ask them each three questions: "What size feet are you?", "Do you have a license?", and "Do you ever go for rides upstate?" Correct answers to those questions were the qualification to be with him. Most of the girls lived in the city and didn't even own a car, let alone go for regular cruises through the countryside. They just lied because he would never know the difference. Once he picked his girl out, he set the scene. He'd take off his clothes other than his shirt and tie, spread the Times out on the floor, and placed a pair of six-inch red stripper heels on the table. Those things were ankle-breakers and shouldn't even be available for purchase, but a lot of the girls were annoyingly good at walking in them! She'd put the heels on and, finding her balance, took a moment to strut around the room. While she warmed up, the good doctor would dig around in his hung-up coat for a small vial. Once located, he'd uncork it and dump a little pile of coke onto the back of his other hand, taking a big inhale of the powder. The girl stood by him, towering over him since he was sitting on the massage table. She used the table to keep her balance, the heels already hurting the balls of her feet. Other girls giggled at the door when the doctor, Gerald, started running through his very predictable script.

"How old were you when you got your license?" he asked, rubbing his hands up and down his thighs.

"Seventeen," she said.

"Do you ever drive upstate?"

"Yeah, pretty often. My aunt lives in Ulster County, so I go up on weekends sometimes to visit her."

Gerald took another hit and smiled. The girl had to continually walk around the room, a feat in and of itself, while she conversed and made up a story on the fly. Gerald started to get hard after that second hit of coke, the excitement spreading through his body. "How fast do you drive?" he said.

"I'm bad, I usually go at least fifty-five even in school zones. I'm not great at following the rules."

"Have you ever hit anything while speeding?"

"Yes. A few times, actually."

"How did it feel?"

"Well, I was driving on a really windy road and this poor little groundhog ran out in front of me, but I was going too fast to stop in time. I tried to swerve, but I hit it."

"Did you go back to see?"

"I had to. The poor creature was totally crushed, its guts were all over the road. I nearly vomited, seeing it like that. I was just crying because I didn't mean to kill it."

Gerald's erection was growing with each passing word. He sniffed coke every couple of minutes during the session, so he must've been pretty high by then.

"What else have you hit?" he asked, stroking himself.

"There's a pretty small town I have to pass through to get to my aunt's. I still speed, even though the limit is like twenty-five. I hit a dog driving through there. A big brown and white one."

"Tell me about it."

"It scared me half to death! When I hit it, it bounced up onto my hood and probably would've broken my windshield if I didn't slam on my breaks."

"Was there blood?"

"The car was covered in it. I think, when I hit it, its head must've slammed into the grill or something, because there was all this goopy stuff left there. And I don't know how, but it was like its body just sort of…burst open. I noticed its intestines were dragged across the pavement, probably because even though I stopped the car as soon as I could, it still went like twenty feet after I hit it."

"Then what," Gerald said rapidly.

"I drove away! I don't know if anyone saw me, but I got out of there as fast as I could, but it was a bad idea. That very same day, I hit something else."

"Really?"

"I wish I was lying. It's like I'm cursed. But it was getting dark out and I could hardly see through my tears. A deer ran out into the road when I was going faster than I had ever gone. I was just trying to get to my aunt's as fast as I could, but I totaled my car hitting that deer. And the brain matter. I'd never seen so much grey stuff. Somehow, it was trying to limp off, but its legs were splayed all weird and half its skull was caved in. I got light-headed when I saw that."

"Oh my god," he moaned.

"The thing died before it was able to drag itself out of the street. I tried to drag its body into the woods, but it was bleeding out so much and it smelled so awful already. I threw up."

Gerald was fully erect and stroking himself rapidly, finishing off the rest of the coke in one long, messy gasp. "Tell me more, about the deer!" he whined.

"The worst part, when I was dragging it, was that the split that had opened up on its belly kept opening more and more until it was basically in two pieces. That's what made me puke."

As she finished her last sentence, the doctor leaned forward and came all over the newspaper. He was out of breath and his face was redder than if he'd been out in the sun for three days, the veins in his eyes bursting. As soon as he was done, he'd fold up the paper and slip it into his portfolio, making space by removing the envelope full of cash. He looked like he'd been dragged through a hedge backward when he passed my desk on his way out. Shockingly, he would schedule his most complicated surgeries for the morning after his coke-fueled roadkill sessions. I bet even if the parents of the kids he operated on knew about his secret, they'd still be lining up for his world-renowned skill. He was often their last hope in saving their children's lives.

# Domme in the Henhouse

Rodger was a weekly caller who had this crazy knack for coming up with the weirdest fetish scenes. In a million years, I couldn't predict what he would come up with next. Naturally, he was a submissive partner who sought out my dommes for his humiliation and roleplay. He had such inane fantasies that I allowed him an exception to speak with the domme he was booking so she could get the script right from him. That way, there was no chance I could water anything down by acting as a middleman. When he'd call, I knew it was him before he said so; he had this distinctive lisp. I wondered if that made it hard for him to be taken seriously as the CEO of a multimillion-dollar corporation, but I suppose it didn't hold him back that much.

This unique incident occurred after we'd been booking Rodger for about a year at that point. He had been with Jaz, our most reliable domme, a few times and he was looking to book her again for his next session. I gave her a call just to make sure she was around, then patched her through so she could speak with Rodger directly. Twenty minutes went by, and I got a call from Jaz, laughing hysterically. She could hardly get the words out and I figured Rodger must've outdone himself this time.

"He wants, he wants me to go," she got out between cackles, "to the costume shop in the West Village and rent a bird costume, extra-large!"

"A bird costume?" I asked, mouth agape.

"Yeah, he said Big Bird or a chicken suit would work, whatever they have in stock!"

"He wants you to wear that?"

"I don't know, I had to hang up before he finished so he wouldn't hear me laughing!"

She was howling on the other end, and I was beginning to crack up, too. A bird costume? What could possibly be hot about that? I was dumbfounded and couldn't imagine what Rodger had in store. I just hoped Jaz would be able to keep it together!

The plan was to meet in a suite not far from the costume shop. It was a good thing it was so close because Jaz had to lug a huge suitcase containing the costume she rented. It wasn't easy to hide because it had some structure to it, giving the wearer that exaggerated, bottom-heavy bird shape. She took the elevator up to Rodger's room and called me before she entered.

"Good luck in there, babe. I'm dying to know how it goes," I said.

"Yeah, I'll let you know," Jaz giggled and hung up.

Rodger let her in before she even had a chance to knock. He was smiling this goofy smile and his cheeks were flushed already, no doubt in anticipation of what he was about to request. The suite was large, with plenty of room for a bird's fluttering about. Like a little boy about to bargain for more dessert, Rodger clasped his hands together and approached Jaz. He's talking and talking, circling to the crux of his request until he goes into the bedroom and brings out a brown paper bag. Inside, there were an array of multi-colored plastic eggs, like the ones used for hiding candy during Easter. There was also a large squeeze bottle of lube. Jaz looked in it, then looked back at Rodger with her eyebrows raised in question.

167

"Okay… so what are we up to today, Rodger?" She asked.

"You brought the costume, right?"

"Yes! Now tell me, what am I going to do with it?"

Rodger perked up even more. He saw the suitcase by the door and hauled it into the bathroom. Jaz heard him moving around in there and heard an excited gasp. He was in there for a few minutes, jumping around and examining himself in the mirror. The unmistakable sound of scissors cutting through fabric piqued Jaz's interest. Annoyance flashed through her as she hoped he wasn't destroying that costume; it was only a rental, and she wouldn't know how to explain what happened. It would definitely be more embarrassing than picking it up in the first place. Suddenly, he came back out to her wearing the costume sans chicken head, shaking with glee. Jaz tried not to burst out laughing, but the man was standing there, holes cut out where his nipples were, and the bottom of the costume cut off entirely. Rodger had also taken the scissors to the bright yellow tights, creating an upside-down "U" shaped opening. The result was a visibly aroused, half-chicken, half-man miscreation with a sidesplitting plan. His unkempt genitals almost made it too much to witness, Jaz told me after the fact.

"I want you to take these," Rodger said, indicating the eggs, "and put them inside me. Then, I'll lay them for you."

Jaz went into domme mode now that the full request had been revealed. "What's in it for me, chickadee?" she asked, crossing her arms.

"I didn't forget, Mistress." Rodger went to a table where his wallet sat. He pulled out a small stack of hundred-dollar bills. He then proceeded to roll-up three at a time and put them in the plastic eggs. They'd be Jaz's reward for a successful laying.

Rodger bent himself over the side of the bed, butt in the air and wagging with anticipation. Jaz lubed up the first egg and slid it up Rodger's backside with ease. He must've been practicing, the thing got lost up there so quickly. The second egg was a similar story, though Rodger released a little grunt as he took it in. Jaz played him, calling him names, and slapping his low-hanging fruit with a solid backhand. Egg number three gave her some trouble, but she got it in even with Rodger protesting and begging for her to be gentle. "Gentle" wasn't exactly in Jaz's vocabulary, so she spanked his ass for whining. His erection twitched as she reprimanded him. A fourth and final egg went in with great effort from both parties, but it only made it halfway before there was no more space left. Rodger gasped and sweated as he took it inside him, feeling the first get pushed further and further back. He could barely stand up; he was so laden with internal agony. He waddled over to a towel that had been set out on the floor and then, as Jaz watched, he started to push.

The egg that was only in halfway, to begin with, came shooting out! Jaz stomped over to Rodger and smacked him across the face, saying how he was being bad since he didn't ask for permission to start laying the eggs. He apologized profusely, his pathetic stance revealing how weak in the knees he was.

"You'll only be allowed to lay more if you're a good boy," she said. Rodger started worshipping her, giving her feet and hands kisses, doing anything to show his appreciation for her. She lavished in the moment, seeing this grown, ridiculously dressed man crawl around on the floor, his butt surely sore from the beating she gave him. She was going to make it worse. She allowed him to lay another but spanked him for bringing plastic to their date.

"Next time," she whispered, "I want eggs made of gold to shove up your tight little ass."

"Yes mistress, I promise, I'll get them for you," he responded. Jaz wasn't kidding either; I'm sure she expected him to not be so frugal the next time he booked with her. She allowed him to push out another egg, the third one so far. It came out with a sticky splat onto the floor, missing the towel.

"Do you intend to clean that up, chicky? You better," Jaz

hollered. He had to be punished again, for making a mess. "Now, you have to strut around the room like the dumb chicken you are, until I'm satisfied. Do it, or you'll have the egg in you till tomorrow!" Rodger clucked and beat his wings, stepping erratically all around the room. Jaz let him do his silly chicken dance for a good five minutes, then clapped for him.

"What a good bird!" she said. "Why don't you come sit on the sofa and show me how good you are at touching yourself. I know you get a lot of practice."

Rodger rushed over to the couch and sidled up to Jaz. He toyed with his member and nearly finished in seconds, but Jaz slapped his hand away. She wanted him to finish as he pushed out the last egg, and he happily obeyed her strict instructions.

Sheer relief washed over the little cock as he came and released the last egg from his stretched-out cavity. He gathered up all his eggs and went to wash them in the bathroom, removing Jaz's $1,200 tip before running them under warm water and giving them a little scrub. Jaz was pleased with the evening's events and couldn't wait to relay what she'd seen with me, as well as a few other domme confidants, I'm sure. She packed up the costume once Rodger had changed out of it and left him to clean up the rest of the room.

"I wish these old jerks would look into some manscaping, at least once in a while! I mean, maybe those eggs would've gone up smoother if they didn't have to get through a forest first!" I was losing it on the other end as Jaz finished telling me the story on her way to return the costume. I hadn't laughed like that in a long, long time. I couldn't imagine how Rodger had come up with this script! Did he have a weird run-in with Big Bird as a child? Was a vibrator just not hitting the spot anymore? I couldn't tell you how it all came to happen, but I can tell you that it did occur, and I was as shocked as you are when I first heard it.

# Afterword

It's such a pleasure to present these short stories to people all over the world who may be curious about my life as a madam. This collection showcases not only my unusual work but the extraordinary appetites of America's richest men. Perhaps the craziest thing about it all is how these pages are not extensive. There is so much more that remains in the shadows, just waiting to be revealed by the light of day. The aftermath and the consequences of operating my business, for example, remain an unspoken topic. The privacy of so many hangs in the balance as I evaluate how best to share the stories that have impacted my life and the lives of my loved ones.

Sharing these stories was the first step on a long path to uncovering all that happened to me during those years as a madam and what happened after. Full of highs and lows, this life has been different, to say the least. Thank you for starting this journey with me.

# Acknowledgments

I want to thank Wahida Clark and her team for making this project happen. I always knew I wanted to share my story with the world, and their support has been a gift. I hope I can continue sharing more and more as time passes. A special thanks to Caroline Zonis for working so closely with me and helping me write this book every step of the way. Finally, thank you to my family; their love motivates me to do great things in my life. I love you all so much. Big kisses!

**WAHIDA CLARK**
**P R E S E N T S**
**INNOVATIVE PUBLISHING**

# AVAILABLE NOW

### FROM WAHIDA CLARK PRESENTS INNOVATIVE PUBLISHING

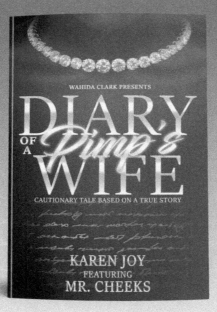

AVAILABLE NOW

WAHIDA CLARK PRESENTS

DIARY
OF A Pimp's
WIFE

CAUTIONARY TALE BASED ON A TRUE STORY

KAREN JOY
FEATURING
MR. CHEEKS

# AVAILABLE NOW

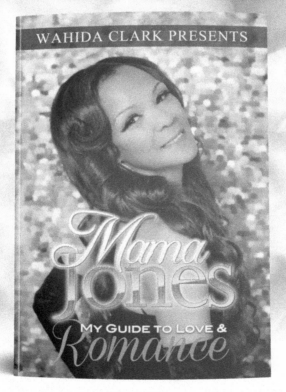

WAHIDA CLARK PRESENTS

Mama Jones

My Guide to Love & Romance

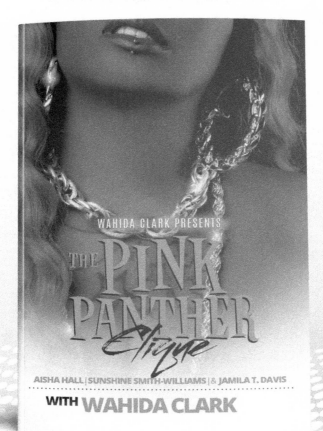

# CLASSIC STREET LIT
## —S—E—R—I—E—S—

FROM WAHIDA CLARK PRESENTS
INNOVATIVE PUBLISHING

CPSIA information can be obtained
at www.ICGtesting.com
Printed in the USA
LVHW110540101022
730326LV00003B/24